Copyright © 2025 by Ankur K. Garg
All rights reserved.
Published in the United States by Youngry Media
623 Morris Avenue, Springfield, NJ 07081
www.youngry.com

Rogue Visionary is a trademark of Ankur K. Garg.
No part of this book may be reproduced, stored in a retrieval system, or transmitted in any form or by any means—electronic, mechanical, photocopying, recording, or otherwise—without written permission from the publisher, except in the case of brief quotations used in reviews, articles, or scholarly work.

Library of Congress Cataloging-in-Publication Data is available upon request.

ISBN 979-8-9936188-0-7
Printed and bound in the United States by On Point Printing, New Jersey.

Book Design by Charlie Leenstra
Cover Photography by Ludwig Araujo
Cover Concept by Ankur K. Garg
Edited by Sean Mabry

10 9 8 7 6 5 4 3 2 1
First Edition

ROGUE
Visionary

**THE HIGHS, LOWS, AND
WAR STORIES OF BUILDING A
$125M BRAND HOUSE—AND
LOSING IT ALL**

Introduction
A Warning

I'll tell you right now, there is no ribbon to tie on the end of this story. No final "lesson learned." No "happily ever after." Because Rogue Visionaries don't land. We launch, again and again. Arrival isn't in our vocabulary. Movement, evolution, and innovation are.

This book isn't a success story. It's a status update.

I'm *still* building. Still betting on instinct. Still choosing clarity over comfort, and pressure over polish. And if I'm being honest…still saying yes more than I say no. That's the real grind. The *every day* unequivocal work ethic. Not the highlight reel, not the Forbes feature, not the valuations. Just the unglamorous, unfiltered zealous pursuit of work that actually *matters*. That's the work that earns attention, drives revenue, and builds communities for brands that people don't just use—they rep like a badge.

It doesn't happen by accident or "luck." It happens because someone had the vision for creating a solution and the grit to make it a reality. The process is not pretty, even if the final result is. It takes people who are bold, direct, and uncompromising, even to the point of going against the grain and butting heads with your team.

And I wouldn't have it any other way. I'd rather be misunderstood than mediocre. I'd rather be intense than invisible. I'd rather burn bright for five years than coast through twenty.

This journey *is not* for everyone. This book isn't meant to be either. In fact, someone asked me recently if I could turn someone into a Rogue Visionary if they aren't one already.

The answer is no. And that probably applies to you too.

If you are not a Rogue Visionary, and you somehow found this book anyway, you will soon put it down and walk away. You will not return to it, and that is for the best. But if you are a Rogue Visionary?

Then this book will be a breath of fresh air.

I'm not here to be your "guru" or "thought leader". I'm here to be your kindred spirit. I'm here to show you what life is like when you abandon all fear. Building sucks. But if you're anything like me, you can't not build. So, let's build bigger. Better. Build things that are real. Build things that matter.

I will tell you what worked for me so you can try it for yourself. I will show you my scars so you can avoid them. And to prove that you and I can both survive catastrophic failure and come back stronger. I will show you how I got here not to score cheap sympathy, but to hold the mirror up to you. Like attracts like, after all. The more my story sounds like yours, the more you'll know what to expect going forward.

So, let's get to work.

Reminder
This is a Memoir

This book is a memoir. While every effort has been made to present events as accurately as possible, memory is a slippery thing—especially when it's filtered through high-stakes deals, sleepless nights, and adrenaline-fueled chapters of entrepreneurship.

Some conversations have been paraphrased or condensed. Certain timelines may be streamlined for clarity. In a few cases, names and identifying details have been changed to protect privacy. And yes—some moments are told with the kind of edge and intensity that only hindsight can provide.

This isn't a court transcript. It's a founder's lens. It's how I lived it, how I saw it, and how I remember it.

If you're looking for perfection, you're reading the wrong book. If you're looking for the truth, even when it's messy, hard, or a little too honest—welcome.

DISCLAIMER

This publication is a work of non-fiction based on the author's personal experiences, recollections, and interpretations. While the events and circumstances described are true to the best of the author's memory, certain details, names, locations, timelines, and dialogues may have been altered, condensed, or reconstructed for narrative flow, clarity, and confidentiality.

The opinions expressed in this book are solely those of the author and do not represent the views or positions of any companies, organizations, or individuals mentioned or referenced. The inclusion of any names or likenesses is not intended to harm, defame, or malign any individual, group, or entity.

This book is not intended to provide business, legal, financial, or medical advice. Readers are encouraged to seek the counsel of licensed professionals before acting on any information presented herein.

Any resemblance to real persons, living or dead, beyond those explicitly referenced, is purely coincidental.

© 2025 Ankur K. Garg. All rights reserved.

Chapter 1
How I Hit My First $1 Million

If you skipped the intro, you might be tempted to read that chapter title and think I'm bragging.

Spoilers: this is the setup to me losing somewhere around $50 million. That would have been generational wealth for a guy like me. My great grandkids wouldn't have had to work. Still, if you haven't hit your first million yet, there's a lesson in here for you. And if you have? *Consider this a useful reminder.*

I hit my first $1 million back when I was co-owner of a sports supplement company called SHREDZ. The other co-owner and the founder was a guy named Arvin Lal who had just had his "15 minutes of fame" on the reality show, *Jersey Shore*. His "in" with the show was that he was best friends with Mike "The Situation" Sorrentino at the time. Then, in classic reality show fashion, he had a six-episode arc where he broke up the show's big couple.

Foreshadowing, I guess? I'll let you be the judge. I barely remember it, to be honest. I didn't watch the show much myself. All I knew was that Arvin was famous. Even if he was only "Jersey famous" that was enough. Despite the show's mixed reputation, there really was a sense of "Jersey pride" surrounding it. Even if the rest of the country only "kinda sorted" remembered Arvin, everyone on our home turf KNEW him. As you'll see, that counted for a lot in the early days.

We met through one of his old fraternity brothers who knew I had a successful marketing agency. He set us up, then Arvin presented me with a logo drawn on a napkin and said, "Can you bring this to life?"

"Hold my beer," I said.

The next day, I sent him the finished logo and blew him away. So then he asked the infamous question, "What else can you do?"

I just had to chuckle and say, "Everything. What do you need me to do?"

Keep in mind, I knew nothing about supplements. So when he asked me to design some labels, I just drove over to a local GNC and studied everything they had on the shelves. I even made up fake UPC codes (at first) because I didn't know what they were.

I should also mention here that this was far from my only gig. I was already running a marketing agency called Crimson Lab where I even had a few Fortune 500 clients. We offered full stack web development along with cutting edge design work. That was my "day job" and by night I was DJing for some of the hottest clubs in New Jersey and New York City. I was no slouch. I didn't "need" Arvin to make a name for myself.

(Why was I so driven already? We'll get to that in the next chapter.)

Still, I saw that Arvin already had one thing that I did not: clout. Everything I was doing back then was a product of pure hustle and grind. I could sell people, sure, but I usually had to get in the room with them first. Or wait for word of mouth to slowly make its way around. Arvin didn't have to do that anymore. Not to the same degree, at least. People were flinging open doors for him that I would have had to kick down by force.

There was still plenty of hustle and grind in our future, of course. But with Arvin's name and face, we could finally make it count. We could build real brand value instead of constantly chasing the next gig. We could force the world to come to *us* instead of us begging *it* for attention.

In our first year, we did about three grand in sales. Total. But that wasn't *just* because we were clueless. It also had to do with the industry. Back then, selling supplements wasn't what it is today. You probably can't imagine a world where you couldn't spin up a Shopify store, throw some ads on Instagram or TikTok, and start shipping tomorrow. But in 2011, that entire playbook didn't exist yet. E-commerce was clunky. Shopify was still in its awkward teenage years. WordPress plugins were buggy. Most "online stores" were nothing more than PayPal "Buy Now" buttons on a static site. Forget one-click checkouts or Apple Pay—people didn't even fully trust putting their credit cards online.

Meanwhile, the supplement industry was stuck in retail quicksand. If you wanted to sell, you had to be on the shelves at GNC, Vitamin Shoppe, or in the local mom-and-pop stores that bodybuilders lived at. That was the system. The gatekeepers were the distributors, the store buyers, the same handful of executives who decided what product got visibility and what product sat in the warehouse until it expired. The playbook was simple: you hired a big-name bodybuilder, slapped their face on your label, bought a booth at the Arnold Classic or Mr. Olympia, and prayed for people to notice. These were not "influencers". These were bodybuilding celebrities. And if you weren't a brand with a major celebrity, there was no place for you in the industry.

So I scraped a list of just under 4,000 supplement stores and I would just call them to talk about SHREDZ. Out of all those stores, we got 12 or 13 to pick us up. They were mostly all local Jersey stores who knew about Arvin from the show. Again, he may not have been a nationwide celebrity, but he *was* a celebrity at home.

That was our first major hit. And even though it didn't do a ton for our bottom line, it at least validated the product.

So instead of banging our heads against the brick wall of retail, we pivoted to something different: creating fitness influencers on Instagram and nurturing communities that we had full control of. Keep in mind: Instagram had just launched in 2010, and it was strictly photography or graphics. No video yet. No Stories. No Reels. No Shop tab. Just square photos with heavy filters that made everything look like a vintage postcard. The entire platform had maybe 5 million users—total. That's less than the number of followers some fitness influencers have *individually* now.

So, when we decided to take a shot on Instagram, it wasn't because it was proven. It was because there was a vibe. The rawness. The immediacy. The fact that people actually cared about what some shredded guy in his garage gym was posting. You could feel the momentum building in real time. Our competition didn't get it. They were still pouring money into glossy magazine ads that no one read or cutting TV spots that aired at 2 a.m. on ESPN2. Meanwhile, we were over here hacking together affiliate funnels for men and women with 5,000 followers who looked like they could deadlift a car.

This was in late 2012, early 2013 when people were just starting to use the term "influencer". SHREDZ was one of the very first companies to bring these influencers on as affiliates. Back before the whole Internet was designed to support that kind of business. Back when we had to build hundreds of individual websites for them. And here's the thing: people in the industry laughed at us. To the old-school supplement execs, Instagram wasn't "serious." Real distribution meant a GNC endcap, not some selfie posted by Joey Swoll. But we saw the flip coming before they did.

Because it wasn't just about where people *bought* their supplements. It was about where people found their identity. And by 2012, identity was starting to shift online. That's why when people ask me now, "How did you guys come up with influencer marketing?" The honest answer is: we didn't *come up with* it. We just paid attention. We saw the cracks forming in the old system, and we decided to drive a truck through them.

On top of that, we also made the whole thing exciting, fun, and profitable *for the influencers.* See, back in my nightlife days, there was this simple system that every club promoter lived and died by: attribution. If you were running a party, you didn't get paid just for showing up with a smile—you got paid when people showed up at the door and dropped your name. "I'm here for Mike." "Put me down for Steve." That's how the club knew who was actually moving bodies through the door. It was crude, it was manual, but it worked.

When Arvin and I looked at Instagram, we realized we could run the same play digitally. Instead of waiting for someone to say a name at a nightclub, we built individual online sales funnels— ~~hundreds~~ thousands of them—so every fitness influencer had their own custom landing page. It sounds obvious now, but back then it was radical. Nobody else in supplements was doing attribution at scale. They were still tossing out 20% off coupon codes and hoping customers remembered to use them. We weren't hoping, we were tracking. Every click, every conversion, every sale had a name attached. And when that sale hit, the influencer got a real-time text alert. We called them "booms." Your phone buzzes, boom! You just made money.

That hit of instant cortisol, aka the cha-ching moment, turned our influencers into obsessed sales machines. They weren't just repping SHREDZ for clout; they were watching their phone light up in real time. And once you've tasted that, once you've seen your name tied to dollars on the spot, you don't go back to old-school "exposure deals." That nightclub trick—just a name at the door—became the backbone of influencer marketing as we know it today.

And it worked. The sales started flowing in like never before.

I even made a little game out of it. "Yo Arvin," I'd say at random points throughout the day, "Fun fact: we just hit X in revenue." Then we'd just laugh and get back to work. With our new influencer strategy and the rush of Black Friday, we managed to close out 2012 at or near $100,000. Still nothing crazy, but it was enough to convince Arvin and I to move in together and go all in on the company SHREDZ.

It was somewhere in early March 2013 when it happened. We were both working in the kitchen when I looked up and said, "Yo Arvin, fun fact…we broke a million dollars in sales."

At first, all we could do was stare at each other.

Finally, he asked, "Should we just keep working?"

"No…" I said, even though I'd had the same thought.

"Should we go out to a club and pop a bottle to celebrate?" he asked.

Again, neither of us liked that idea either. So instead, I went over to our Nespresso machine and made us two shots of espresso. Then we downed those to celebrate and got back to work.

As SHREDZ grew, and grew its team, that became our tradition. Later on when we hit $10 million, I went to Starbucks and ordered 47 shots of espresso for everyone on the team. Then we gathered everyone around, told them the story behind it…and they just looked at us like we were crazy. Maybe we were. But maybe you kind of get it. Maybe you can even imagine yourself doing the same thing.

Either way, I'm sure you're curious about where I got the idea. Why my first instinct was "keep working" after hitting a milestone most people can't even imagine. To answer that, we're going to have to put the story of SHREDZ on pause.

We'll come back to it, since we built it up to a $125 million brand house before I lost it all.

For now, though, let's go back to the very beginning.

Chapter 2
Why I Pushed Past My First $1 Million

Have you ever heard of Ankur Garg?

No, not me. I'm Ankur K. Garg, like it says on the cover. Right now, we're talking about Ankur Garg, one of the biggest film producers in India. The irony of us having the same name runs deep. It's a perfect example of what I want to talk about here: why money is important, but *power* is the real goal.

In case you haven't guessed by now, I'm Indian too. I was born in Lucknow, India, and my parents immigrated to the US in 1985 when I was just a little kid. I like to joke that my parents didn't immigrate for opportunity—they immigrated because the **prince was born**. That's what they told everyone in Lucknow when I showed up. My mom literally said, *"The prince has arrived. We must take him to America."*

We first landed in Texas and moved in with my dad's older brother. By that point, he was a full-on Texas man—cigarettes in one hand, belt buckle the size of a dinner plate, married to a kind American woman who didn't speak a word of Hindi. I was a kid watching my parents navigate this wild contrast: Indian roots in a cowboy environment. Imagine two highly educated immigrants, trying to reorient their entire lives inside a family unit that had already assimilated.

Soon after that, we moved out to Queens, NY and all shared a one-bedroom studio apartment, while they worked multiple jobs. My dad went back to school. He got into NYIT for computer science—because tech was booming and it was the clearest shot to building a new life. This is a guy who already had a full academic resume, starting over because no one here cared about his Indian degrees. My mom—who managed finances like a pro back home—took a cashier job at a local grocery store.

And then came the language barrier—not just speaking English but understanding how America worked. The slang, the culture, the hidden rules. Everything from how you talk to a teacher to how you buy groceries was different. My parents weren't clueless—they were just decoding in real-time. Every form, every phone call, every piece of mail was a translation project.

As a kid, I didn't have the words for it—but I *felt* it every day. The way my house smelled. The clothes I wore. The food I brought to school. Everything about me felt a little "other." It wasn't bad—it was just… obvious. I remember opening lunchboxes and realizing really fast that my meals weren't anything like what the other kids had. No PB&J. No Capri Sun. No Lunchables. I had homemade parathas, sabzi, sometimes even dal in a Thermos. Food that would be five-star on Yelp today, but back then just made me feel different. Funny thing is, I didn't know how good I had it until I got older. My grandmother was a phenomenal chef. My mom had actual culinary training. I was eating better than 90% of the kids in the cafeteria—I just didn't know it because it didn't *look* American.

I wasn't embarrassed—I was just observant. I noticed the gap between my world and theirs. My classmates had a structure to their lives I didn't understand. Nicer bikes. American idioms. Parents on school boards. Summer camps. I had chores, rules, and a deep understanding of how much my parents were sacrificing behind the scenes. Speaking of summer, that's where my parents' real ingenuity came in. Every summer, they'd send me to live with my aunt in Delaware. Not because they didn't want me around—but because childcare and summer activities weren't in the budget. It was a brilliant, pragmatic solution: save money on daycare and let me grow up around family.

Those summers were formative. I bonded with my cousins. I got to see a different version of American life. But more than anything, I learned the quiet genius of how immigrant families operate. No waste. No fluff. Just resourceful, strategic decisions designed to build momentum without burning out. My parents and extended family didn't make it in America by outworking everyone. They made it by outlasting the pressure—and never letting pride get in the way of progress.

For the record, this is why I don't consider my life a "rags to riches" story at all. My parents did what they had to not just make ends meet but create better opportunities for all of us. In fact, my mom understood this on a whole different level, which we'll get to in a moment. They *were* successful back in India. My mom was essentially a CPA and, like I said, my dad had a degree in advanced mathematics. They were respected, educated, and deeply rooted in their community. But they also knew the reality: no matter how hard they worked, the ceiling was low and the system was rigid. If you weren't from the "right" family or didn't fit neatly into one of a few accepted professional tracks, your career—and your lifestyle—had limits. (Care to guess which kind of family the *other* Ankur Garg came from?)

All this gave me a foundational identity: I was taught to listen more than I speak. To respect elders. To stay sharp in rooms that didn't look like me, didn't sound like me, and didn't always welcome me. That deep connection to family—extended family especially—wasn't a cultural formality. It was the infrastructure. A built-in support system made up of aunties, uncles, cousins, and community that created safety even when money was tight.

But that same infrastructure came with invisible ceilings. The cultural script was clear: study hard, play it safe, get a respectable job. That was the expectation.

I wanted more. Not out of rebellion, but out of *hunger*. I didn't want to maintain stability—I wanted to create *freedom*. Growing up as an only child, I always had this deep sense that I had potential, which only intensified my desire to break out. I just thought I needed the right person to come along and elevate that potential. Even then, I understood you could *earn* money, but you had to be *given* fame. I wanted someone to come and give me that.

They never did. *Instead*, I had to work to prove myself.

Case in point, when I was in high school, I had all these grand visions of going to a prestigious college. I knew I needed volunteer credits, so on top of excelling in school, working as a DJ, and selling weed (we'll get to that) I also volunteered with Operation Smile.

In case you haven't heard of it, Operation Smile is a well-respected nonprofit that's still in operation to this day. Their mission is to provide surgery to children born with a cleft palate. That's where the name comes from. They find children who literally cannot smile and give them the ability to do so.

That blew my mind as a teenager. For two reasons.

On the lighter side, I was so impressed with the generosity of the organization. Everyone from the doctors performing surgeries, the teens volunteering like me, even the administrators it takes to manage it all. All these people giving their time and money to help these kids when they could be doing literally anything else. It's beautiful.

On the darker side, I couldn't help but wonder why these kids had to be born with cleft palates to begin with. All I could think was that God made a mistake. What else do you call a child that can't smile?

So I decided I was going to use my potential to fix God's mistakes. I was going to become one of those doctors. That was my roadmap.

Now, look, I know I just said I come from immigrant parents. *Indian* parents. Is it possible they planted the idea of becoming a doctor in my head? Yes, of course they did. But, like I said, my mom took this to a different level. See, when it came time for me to apply for colleges, my dad had just been laid off. Money was tight, so I had to go to my guidance counselor and play the numbers game. I ended up paying out of pocket to apply to two schools then got state grants to apply to another five.

If just getting into college was such a long shot, what were my odds of becoming a doctor?

My mom understood this, so one night she sat me down and asked, "Why do you want to be a doctor?" She nodded along as I talked about fixing God's mistakes, then she asked, "How many people can a doctor help in an hour?"

"Probably one, maybe two at best," I said.

"Okay, then how many people can a hospital help in an hour?"

Then we *really* played the numbers game. As best as we could, we sat and calculated the costs of building, maintaining, and operating a hospital. That's when something shifted in me. That's when I saw the true value, and power, of money.

To be clear, I already had an entrepreneurial streak in me. Remember Ankur Garg? The other one? Well, at one point in high school I noticed he owned the website domain for *our* name. As a budding web developer, I wanted to own the domain for my own name. So, I figured out how to reach out to him…and he quoted me $10,000 to buy the domain.

At first, I couldn't even imagine how to get that kind of money. I was already making *some* money as a DJ, but not that kind of money. Still, I had already discovered one of my all-time favorite quotes:

"Aut inveniam viam aut faciam."

That roughly translates as "I will find a way or I will make one." Legend has it, that's what the Carthaginian general Hannibal said when everyone around him said it was "impossible" to bring his elephant cavalry through the Alps. Spoilers for 218 BC: He did, and it's still one of the greatest military triumphs in history.

Anyway, in my effort to "make a way" to raise $10,000, I wound up dealing weed. Mind you, this was way *way* before legalization. If I had gotten caught, it could have completely destroyed my college plans. Still, despite all the risk and anxiety, I pulled together the $10,000.

And then Ankur Garg refused to sell me the domain. Still.

As much as that experience stung, it was a major lesson in what I was capable of. And when I had that fateful conversation with my mom, I realized I could apply that same power to something greater than myself. I'm no saint, for the record. Soon after that, I watched the movie *Boiler Room* with one of my friends and fell in love with it. That's when I decided to become a finance broker and use *my* money to build hospitals…and also have a ton of fun along the way.

Still, when I think back on that conversation with my mom—the one about doctors and hospitals—it strikes me how subtle she was about it. She didn't hand me a roadmap; she handed me a lens. She never said don't chase purpose. She just refused to let me confuse purpose with prescription. That's the trap most ambitious people fall into—mistaking the label for the mission. I thought "doctor" meant "healer." What she really taught me was that healing could take a thousand forms. Some people use scalpels. Some use spreadsheets. Some use stories.

For a long time, I thought rebellion meant doing the opposite of what my parents wanted. Turns out, it meant understanding what they actually meant. They didn't want stability for me—they wanted sovereignty. They didn't want safety—they wanted sustainability. And that's a whole different game. So, when people talk about "finding their why," I smile. I didn't have to find mine. It found me at a kitchen table in a one-bedroom apartment, when my mother looked me in the eye and challenged me to think bigger than a paycheck or a title.

That's what purpose really is: not what you're told to do, but what you're trusted to become. And that trust—hers, mine, yours—is the most valuable capital you'll ever earn.

Easy to say now, of course. My "why" back then was a lot simpler, if less sophisticated: money, power, and fixing God's mistakes. That's what drove me to our first $1 million at SHREDZ. Then it drove me way past that point. It's why I pounded the espresso instead of popping champagne. Why I kept working. Then. Now. Always.

But the real test was waiting for me at the $125 million mark.

Chapter 3
Building a $125 Million Brand House

People love to talk about "overnight success." They say it with a kind of envy that sounds like admiration. They don't mention that the "night" lasts a good five years or more. It's also not the kind of night you sleep through.

Mine started in a two-bedroom apartment that doubled as a warehouse. We had fat burner tubs stacked to the ceiling, labels curling off the corners from the humidity, and two MacBooks that ran so hot they could've doubled as space heaters. Arvin and I would pull eighteen-hour days with the blinds shut, surviving on protein shakes, Nespresso, and momentum. That's the part nobody sees in the highlight reels. Before the millions, before the headlines, before the envy—there's just you, a screen, and the decision to stay awake a little longer than everyone else.

That's how we survived the long, slow, brutal climb to our first $100,000 by the end of 2012. Really, we owed most of that to the Black Friday and our newly discovered influencer model. Back then, the word "influencer" wasn't in the business playbook yet. Instagram was still wild territory. Nobody was talking about affiliate codes and landing pages like they do now. We were inventing it on the fly.

Like I hinted at earlier, I built a system where every influencer got their own funnel. If you were a fan of a yoga teacher, you didn't land on some generic SHREDZ site—you landed on a funnel that reflected that vibe. Same if you were a Cross Fitter, a powerlifter, or a guy who just wanted abs for summer. We took it down to the tiniest details. If Joey Swoll was your guy, when you bought the Alpha Male Stack SHREDZ, you didn't just get a supplement—you got a thank-you email signed by Joey himself. That personal touch turned clicks into conversions.

How'd we even think of that? Instinct. How did we know it would work? By rapid, ruthless testing and listening to the data. Make no mistake, you need both.

Case in point, in the first quarter of 2012 did a deep dive into the fat burner market and discovered something shocking (at least to us): Women were the real buyers. They didn't just want to get "shredded." They wanted a fat burner formulated for them. Cue the montage of me opening my MacBook Pro and creating the very first Pink label and adjusting the targeted copy. Then, Arvin and I carefully removed the labels from 100 jars of the fat burner (you know, the original gold labels that were definitely designed for men) and knowing that our formula was also safe for women, we applied pink labels and launched our Female Fat Burner on Instagram. Well, suffice it to say, women want products made with them in mind. So we made that pivot and our sales skyrocketed.

Of course, we didn't just stop at re-labeling our existing products. Once we had validated the new direction, we reached out to our manufacturers and created a unique women-targeted formula and eventually two entirely unique product lines and stacks. Still, I want to put this in perspective so you can really appreciate how quickly things changed… My "fun fact" for Arvin that month was, "We're selling 19 Alpha Female Stacks for every 1 Male unit."

At that point, Arvin looked at me shocked and responded, "That's like selling 19 AMG cars for every C300 at a Mercedes-Benz dealership." Our average ticket was over $125. We had lightning in a bottle.

By the way, do you want to know the #1 barrier to growing a supplement brand? It's not the product itself. It's not the label design. It's not even which influencers you attach. Obviously, those things are important too, but your competition can copy all that in an afternoon. In fact, our competitors did just that. They didn't even try to hide it. I kept hearing through the grapevine that they'd sit in boardrooms, pull up our Instagram page, and just say, "Copy that."

That was pointless, of course. We created faster than they could copy. We also dug into the data and seized the opportunities they couldn't (or wouldn't) see. This brings me back to the #1 barrier to growing a supplement brand: getting people to actually *open the thing*. That's the main reason why people don't buy more of a supplement after the initial purchase.

How is ANY business supposed to grow and stay competitive without repeat customers?

So unlike all the other supplement brands, we focused on changing that. Sometimes that meant adding a personal touch, like that Joey Swoll email I mentioned earlier. We started doing Skype video calls with the customers and showing them how to make their first protein shake. Engaging with customers in private Kik channels, Instagram engagement pods, and WhatsApp groups. Sometimes, it even meant bundling in other offers like workout guides or cookbooks. We would do anything just to get them actually using the product, because we knew that gave us a massive competitive edge.

It worked. By the time we peaked, SHREDZ was producing mid 8 figures in revenue per year with over 2000 macro and micro influencers on payroll.

I didn't sleep much. I'd go six or seven days straight on pure adrenaline and caffeine, crash for 48 hours, then wake up and do it again. Every part of me was wired to grow. And the world noticed. Everywhere I went—Miami, LA, New York—I'd see people in SHREDZ shirts. Sometimes I'd just sit back and watch someone walk by wearing our brand like a badge. *Surreal doesn't even begin to cover it.*

I remember one time rushing through Newark airport to make it on a flight to Florida. This was for a meeting with a potentially massive client for us. (Let's just say she used to be married to Ben Affleck, and her manager was the inspiration for *The Fresh Prince of Bel Air*) So, of course, Arvin and I—two Punjabi men with beards—start sweating bullets trying to get through security on time.

Right then, one of the TSA guys screams our names. My first thought is, "Oh shit, they just see two brown dudes with beards flying to Miami and think something's up." Remember, this is still in the mid 2010s.

But then…why did they know our names?

Turns out, they were calling to walk us *past* security. Like, completely past. No luggage scan, no taking our shoes off, nothing. That blew my mind…but then again, we were flying out to meet Jenny from the block. Maybe her people had something to do with it, or *maybe* it was us.

Money was moving so fast we could barely keep track of it. But we were still frugal and we didn't even pay ourselves yet. We turned massive penthouses in the largest Jersey City residential compound into our office spaces. Oh, you want to stop me here and say you can't do that? Well, we rented 40+ apartments in the luxury apartment complex so every member of our team could live on-site. The complex couldn't even say anything because everyone had keys and elevator cards to get around!

That was our version of Silicon Valley perks: free housing, espresso on tap, and twenty-hour workdays. When we expanded west, we did the same thing in Orange County—two penthouses that doubled as both corporate HQ and content studio. We built a place where athletes, editors, photographers, and managers could live, train, and shoot without ever leaving the building.

People think that idea came from influencer culture, but it actually came from logistics. Shipping from New Jersey to California was bleeding money, and the best talent was already in LA. So we built what we needed—a talent house before "content house" was even a term. Inside, you'd see world-class bodybuilders editing footage at 2 a.m., social media teams scheduling posts next to a stack of dumbbells, and athletes FaceTiming fans between photo shoots. HR nightmares? Maybe. But for a while, it worked.

We weren't trying to build a company that looked like Google; we were trying to build a company that *moved* like music—fast, loud, a little chaotic, but perfectly in rhythm. The line between home and hustle disappeared, and so did the distance between creator and brand. That's what made it magic… and eventually, what made it fragile.

At one point, across all our accounts and influencer networks, we ~~reached~~ controlled nearly 100 million followers. We opened domestic offices in Jersey City, NJ and Santa Ana, CA; shortly followed by international officers in Beverwijk, Netherlands, and Melbourne, Australia. We spun off ventures like Flavor God Seasonings, Skinny Bunny Tea, and so many more. We even started consulting as "ghost-marketers" for national brands that I can't even tell you about because of permanent NDAs I had to sign.

At the peak, I calculated our cost to acquire a customer—about $1.35. In consumer-packaged goods, that number was unheard of. Joey Swoll alone was pulling in six figures a month just from his SHREDZ deal. It felt like we'd hacked the system.

But here's the thing about rocket ships: they don't coast. They either keep climbing or they blow apart. Behind the big, brassy numbers, cracks were forming. Up to that point, I'd built everything on instinct—velocity over structure, charisma over policy. If something broke, I fixed it. If a sale stalled, I rewrote the copy myself. It worked…right up until it didn't.

The part that worked is exactly what makes it so hard to change: working the way I did was great for morale. Everyone on the team could see how hard I was working. Most people have a built-in instinct to keep pace with others. Nobody wants to be the weak link. And for top talent? They just get more competitive the more things heat up. And nobody has a bigger influence on that than the C-suite. One way or another, every move you make sets an example for every single person in the organization.

Of course that leads directly to the part that *didn't* work: me becoming the bottleneck. Worse, I was setting a negative example for the team. Sure, my work ethic was great, but I was showing them that it's *normal* to become the bottleneck and let things pile up. How was anyone in management supposed to actually *manage* if they were just doing other people's work for them?

So, I went from being the guy who made everything happen to the guy who had to make everything **documented.** Every process suddenly needed an SOP—how returns were handled, how labels were printed, even what temperature the warehouse had to stay at. Was it my favorite thing to do? Nope. In fact, it took me a while to break the habit of relying on instinct for everything. Not that I gave up on instinct entirely, mind you. I just made sure I was saving it for the challenges that mattered most.

Because when those challenges came, it took everything I had to keep a handle on them. The lawsuits. Prop 65 compliance. The endless law firms on retainer. Even Instagram itself was shifting under our feet. And honestly, I wish I could say it was one of those things that took us out. That would almost be easier to admit.

But it wasn't any of those things. We probably could have handled all that and more except for the real problem. In fact, for quite a while there, we did.

Chapter 4
Lawsuits, Prop 65, and 12 Law Firms on Retainer

Here's the part they don't tell you about building a nine-figure brand: the bigger you get, the bigger a target you become.

When you're small, nobody cares. You can mess up, pivot, test, fail. The spotlight isn't on you. But once you're visible? Once you start making real money? The predators come out. At SHREDZ' peak, it felt like every week came with a new letter. Certified mail. Legal notices. Some "urgent matter" that required immediate attention. And there was one phrase that, to this day, sends a shiver down my spine.

Prop 65.

If you don't know, it's a California law that requires warning labels on any product that contains certain chemicals—even in trace amounts, even if they pose no real health risk. On paper, it's about protecting consumers. To be clear: I'm not saying that consumers don't deserve protection. I'm saying the way Prop 65 is enforced makes no sense at all. The way it's worded means that almost *any* product you sell in California requires the warning.

The result? Those little yellow diamonds appear on everything, and most Californians just tune them out. Why bother checking for the warning if it's on everything? Not to mention the fact that anything that Prop 65 is there to warn you about is already present in the water supply. The Prop 65 list isn't ten or twenty items—it's over nine hundred. Everything from lead and arsenic to BPA and even acrylamide, the compound formed when you toast bread. In California, you can't even buy a cup of coffee without a cancer warning. Especially because there are *naturally occurring* amounts of certain heavy metals in everything from the soil to plants and animals that still fall above the Prop 65 threshold. *You* would probably need a Prop 65 sticker if you were a product being sold in California, no matter how clean you eat or how well you cleanse. That's not safety—that's noise.

Besides, just imagine if you don't live in California and you see one of these warnings on the bottle "this product may cause cancer!"

So in practice, Prop 65 does practically nothing to protect consumers. Instead, it creates a goldmine for lawyers. All they have to do is test a product, claim it violates Prop 65, and file a lawsuit. They know you'll settle, because fighting costs more than paying them off. We were a perfect target: big, loud, profitable, and young enough as a company that they thought we didn't know how to defend ourselves.

Of course, you might be wondering why we'd still include the Prop 65 label for customers living outside of California. The answer is that anything else would have been a logistical nightmare. Shipping products with and without that label would have meant tracking separate inventories for every single SKU, state, and warehouse—tens of thousands of moving parts. One missing sticker and suddenly you're facing a recall, a fine, or worse, a class-action lawsuit. So instead, we made the call every smart operator eventually has to make: protect the business first. One unified label meant one unified system.

Even still, that only did so much to protect us. There were still slip-ups. The letters still came. One after another.

We started with one law firm. Then two. Then three. Before long, we had twelve law firms on retainer. Twelve. Just to handle the constant stream of lawsuits, compliance questions, and regulatory landmines. That's not a flex. That's insanity.

Think about what that does to a business. Instead of using cash to innovate, you're burning it on lawyers. Instead of building, you're defending. Instead of focusing on customers, you're sitting in conference rooms arguing about technicalities. And every dollar that goes to legal fees is a dollar that doesn't go into growth.

The emotional cost was worse. Imagine opening your email and wondering which lawsuit was waiting today. Imagine trying to inspire a team while knowing half your calendar is now spent in depositions and legal reviews. Imagine waking up at 3 a.m. with one thought: *What if this is the one that kills us?*

I felt like I was running a law firm disguised as a supplement company. Every leadership meeting started to sound the same: risk, compliance, liability. My role shifted from growth to defense. From CEO to firefighter. And when you spend that much time on defense, your foundation starts to crack. Inside the company, people felt the tension. Some worried their jobs weren't safe. Some worried we'd sell out. Some thought we'd collapse under the weight.

The worst part wasn't even fear—it was shame.

My parents came to this country ready to start all over, worked double shifts, and somehow never complained. Meanwhile, here I was, running a multi-million-dollar company, and I couldn't breathe under the weight of it. I kept thinking, *they crossed an ocean for me to build something. I can't be the one who lets it fall apart over paperwork.*

That's the part nobody prepares you for. Success doesn't just test your ideas—it tests your nervous system. By that point, I wasn't running a business anymore. I was running on fumes and cortisol.

In case you're wondering, this is not some pity party. This is the reality of what it means to be a Rogue Visionary.

At $1 million, you're invisible. At $10 million, you get noticed. At $100 million, it's open season. Every dollar in sales buys you another lawyer's attention. This is true of every industry in the world. If it's not Prop 65 then it's something else. Make no mistake: this has nothing to do with how good your product is. It has nothing to do with how good a person you are. None of these lawyers care about any of that. Their job is to find and exploit cracks in the law to bring lawsuits against companies with deep pockets. That's it. That's how they get paid, and there will always be cracks in the law for them to exploit.

Is that "discouraging"? Do you wish it wasn't so? Too bad. You can wish all you want, just like I do. But wishing for the law to change is not going to build your vision. One way or another, these are the battles you must be ready to fight.

In fact, that should be your test. Do you think your vision is worth all this? Are you willing to go through this kind of pressure to build it? If not, then why bother?

As stressful as it was, I never saw the lawsuits as an excuse to walk away. They were merely the price of doing business. I took pride, if not joy, in our ability to fight through them and keep growing. After all, that's what every other 9-figure company has had to do. And if it had just been the lawsuits, we probably would've survived.

Same goes for the Instagram algorithm, by the way. Around this same time, Instagram was going through its own upheaval. Part of it was that there were just way more influencers competing for the same eyeballs. Now that we'd proven the model, everyone with a physique and some on-camera charm wanted their piece.

But the real shift came in 2016, when Facebook started remaking Instagram in its own image. Between the switch to an engagement-based algorithm, the push for more Stories, and the focus on selling ad space, Instagram was changing fast. What was once our "blue ocean" was rapidly being commoditized and walled off in favor of pushing paid media.

Inside the office, it felt like a code-red situation. My phone buzzed nonstop—managers texting screenshots of collapsing analytics, influencers calling in panic because their reach was down 80 percent. We ran emergency meetings trying to reverse-engineer what the hell Facebook had changed this time. Every theory sounded plausible and every fix felt obsolete by morning.

The truth was simple: Instagram had stopped being a community and started being a casino. The house—Facebook—was taking its cut. The new engagement-based feed meant only the top few percent of posts got oxygen. Everyone else had to pay for ads just to talk to their own audience. Emotionally, it was brutal. For years, we'd lived on the dopamine of instant feedback—likes, comments, shares, and most of all "booms". That was our pulse. Both for us and our influencers. And now it was slipping away. Watching those numbers fall felt like watching your heart rate flatline on a monitor.

I remember standing in front of the whiteboard during one of those all-hands meetings, staring at the words *paid media strategy*. I realized we didn't own our audience—we were renting it. And our landlord had just raised the rent. The irony? We had built the influencer economy, and the very platform we helped legitimize was now pricing us out of it.

Again, none of this is particularly surprising in retrospect. Facebook is a business, and a publicly traded one at that. Its job is to make as much money as possible. The transformation of Instagram certainly accomplished that.

Still, this is another good lesson in the power of clout. For all the money we had made from and *for* Instagram, we didn't own it. Mark Zuckerberg did. He could do whatever he wanted with it and still can to this day. You might have noticed that people aren't looking at social media with rose-tinted glasses anymore. For a number of reasons. Facebook and Instagram especially. And yet, the machine keeps running and people keep paying Zuckerberg for access to other people's eyeballs. They're getting a worse deal on those eyeballs year after year, but too bad. Zuckerberg owns them, and he can charge whatever price he wants.

The reality is, we could have survived that too. I know plenty of people who did. You should be prepared to face similar disruptions as a Rogue Visionary. Frankly, you should be prepared to play the game even when it's not fair. For all the legitimate criticisms we could make of Meta and social media in general, this system is *still* more flexible than what my parents left behind in India. At least you *can* buy your way in here. At least you *can* get creative and hack the system for your benefit. At least you *can* innovate and expand your business. We were doing all that and more, even if it felt like little more than treading water at the time.

No, the real threat to SHREDZ wasn't coming from the outside. It was coming from inside the penthouse. And it was something that was there from the very beginning, just waiting to go off like a ticking time bomb.

For the record here is the loophole for Prop 65, that cost me tens of thousands of dollars to learn…

It only applies if the company that owns the product line has 10 or more employees.

So, you can tell that ambulance chasing fake law-firm to screw off if you have less than 9 employees OR if you know how to set up corporate structures.

You're Welcome

Chapter 5
Losing $50 Million

Imagine this for a second...

You're running a company with over 40 team members all under the same roof. You come in, first thing in the morning, and notice about half of them wearing t-shirts that say "Team [Your Name]".

How would that make you feel? Special? Excited? Validated?

Let me tell you...when I first walked into the office and saw that exact same thing, I hated it. Don't get me wrong, I was flattered to see how much those team members believed in me. The problem is that they weren't just supporting me, they were taking a side.

The other side? Team Arvin. And no, they didn't have t-shirts, but they had their own badge of honor: fat commission checks and millions of followers. If that sounds like a dangerous imbalance of power, it was. Those influencers were the ones who brought in sales, AKA the lifeblood of the business. In fact, they were arguably the "face" of SHREDZ even more so than Arvin at that point. He still made plenty of public appearances, but people weren't buying their supplements directly from him. In their minds, they were buying them directly from Joey Swoll or Paige Hathaway.

Meanwhile, the "Team AKG" crew? They were the only reason the influencers had products to sell in the first place. They were the ones coding and maintaining websites for them, managing logistics, designing labels, and everything else it took to create an appealing product and deliver it to paying customers. Their roles may not have been as glamorous as what the influencers were doing, but they were just as essential. So for these two camps to go to war? It was like an autoimmune disease for the business. Two systems attacking each other when each one literally depended on the other one for survival. Not good.

At the time, I was too focused on putting out all those fires I mentioned in the last chapter to really process it. Looking back, that has to be the first major sign that SHREDZ wasn't just in trouble, it was doomed. People like to talk about "company culture" as if it's this fluffy little thing. Lavish team retreats, "company values" on big posters, and beer in the breakroom. Honestly, even our team penthouses were an example of this, even though they also had practical value.

That's not culture. That's bribing your team to like you.

Wait, but what about our tradition of taking espresso shots together? Yeah, that was long gone by this point. For one thing, the last thing anyone needed at that point was more energy. Everyone was so on edge that adding extra caffeine to the mix was liable to cause violence, panic attacks, or both. Besides, revenue was becoming an increasingly awkward conversation. We weren't hitting milestones at nearly the same pace as before. At a certain point, we decided it was best for morale not to say anything…or, at least, that's how we hoped to protect the last dregs of morale we had left.

No, the real test of "company culture" is if your people identify WITH the company. If they do, then you can come together and move mountains. If you don't then everything becomes an uphill battle. That's why the t-shirt gang vs. the influencers was an ill-omen. They showed that the team was identifying with us as individual leaders. They didn't see us all working together for the good of SHREDZ.

Truth be told, we weren't anymore.

I'd always believed co-founders should balance each other out. I still do, in fact. You don't need to be the same—you need to be complementary. I handled brand, growth, and operations. Arvin had celebrity, charisma, and a following from Jersey Shore. At first, it worked. He was the face. I was the engine. Together, we made things happen. Everything we touched turned to gold. After a while, it was hard to imagine we could *ever* stop working so well together. The only problem was, we were both running on instinct, and we never took the time to make sure our instincts were aligned.

As Instagram changed and the business required just as much defense and offense, our differences only became more obvious.

It got so bad that we literally stopped talking to each other *for years.* How were we supposed to have a unified vision for the company if we weren't even talking to each other?

More than anything, that is the thing that destroyed SHREDZ. That is why our growth was slowing down, and everything became so hard. That's why the stress between us filtered down into the team and forced them to pick sides. My personal stress got so bad that *half my mustache disappeared.* Seriously. I have a rare form of alopecia that flares up in random spots when my stress gets bad enough. I even got one of those little markers that barbers use to fill in the gaps in a guy's beard and used it every day.

The breaking point came when a buyer showed up. A real exit. My cut would have been around $30 Million before taxes. For me, that would have been life-changing money. A chance to cash out, reset, and maybe even protect the brand by letting a larger player handle the next stage of growth. Not just for me, by the way. There were other team members with equity stakes who could've gotten a nice little payout too. Not as Arvin and I would have gotten, but maybe enough to start a kid's college fund or throw towards a down payment on a house. And what about all the early and mid-career team members? Under new leadership, they might have finally had a chance to climb the ladder instead of wading through the toxic swamp.

I wanted to take it. I would have…if not for one mistake I made years ago.

Way back when I'd first jumped from a 15% stake to a 41% stake, Arvin insisted on 1) taking a ½ percent from me in exchange for being the one who opened the $5000 credit card that started it all, which I found annoying but approved, and 2) adding a specific clause to our operating agreement. That clause would give him full veto power on any deal to sell the company.

So, when we had this buyout on the table, Arvin said no.

"It's 9 figures or we're not selling."

Was it runaway ego? Spite? Doesn't matter. Didn't matter then, certainly. Even though we'd built this company together, even though we'd given pieces of equity to all these other key players, that was it. No deal. That's when I realized there was no future for SHREDZ. The one guy who could make or break everything wasn't thinking straight.

What proceeded from there was real animosity between us, the kind of stuff they write movies about, and the only solution was to start treating revenue centers as individual silos. I kept innovating and building new revenue silos, but, after they hit a certain threshold, they would be taken away from me. Then I would be told to build another new revenue stream. *Again.* This was wildly exhausting, but the biggest part of the business didn't have me involved anymore, and a mistake in an 8 figure revenue year costs millions.

I had tunnel vision on saving what was my biggest success in life so far. I borrowed money, put my name on the line, forewent getting a salary so we could pay bills, and sacrificed every resource I had to try and save the company…but I couldn't save the company alone.

So, in 2017, after finding out my partners hated me and were lying to me for months/years to try and get me out of the company, I did the hardest thing I've ever had to do in my life. I walked away. From the penthouse. From the brand. From the team I'd bled for. I didn't walk away rich. I walked away broke. Even though the company *did* eventually buy my shares after years of arbitration, it was for pennies compared to that old deal Arvin vetoed. Worse, they structured my payouts so that I would only get breadcrumbs for the first *five years* after the sale, then I'd get my "big" payouts later on. Forget living off that money, it was barely enough to clean up all the personal debt I'd taken on trying to save the business.

The hardest part wasn't losing the money, though. It was losing myself.

For years, SHREDZ had been my identity. The first thing people asked me about. The proof that an immigrant kid from Jersey could build an empire. When it collapsed, I didn't just lose a company—*I lost who I thought I was.*

But you know what I recognize now, looking back?

I was the only one who had the power to save the company. That responsibility was solely, 100% mine.

Yep. Not Arvin's. Mine. I let him add that clause to our operating agreement to give him veto power. Honestly, looking back I'm sure he would have come around if I pushed back on it. Instead, I eventually let our differences come between us instead of continuing to be the bigger man. I let our toxicity ooze out into the entire company. And as a Rogue Visionary, I can't look back and place the blame anywhere else. If I did, I'd be declaring that I'm *not* a Rogue Visionary.

I played a specific role in the downfall, and I had to accept the status quo. I made the decisions I made. I have the scar tissue to prove it. Am I disappointed in how other people behaved? Absolutely. But my feelings on the matter do not change reality. As we'll get to in a later chapter, this permanently changed how I do business. Though I still believe partnerships are essential, I'm not naive about how I set them up anymore. I don't hand out ownership just to bribe people to stay.

I take responsibility for everything, and everyone, all the time. That does not mean I micromanage, nor does it mean I try to do everything myself. It means that, when something goes wrong, I accept that I was the cause one way or another. And then I go and fix it.

I also choose to have heart, and to have faith in humanity. Honestly, even after all this, there's a part of me that still misses working with Arvin. Sometimes I wonder if he feels that way too. Looking back, I don't think either of us wanted to destroy the other. We were both trying to protect what we'd built. We just couldn't agree on what that meant anymore. For him, protection meant control. For me, it meant freedom.

By definition, betrayal doesn't come from an enemy. **It comes from people who once swore they'd never hurt you.**

We'd built this company side by side—same ambition, same grind, same sleepless nights. But success changes people. It changes *what they see when they look at you.* Once ego gets involved, logic is useless. Every conversation becomes a courtroom. Every suggestion sounds like an accusation. You start counting how many times you've been right just to prove you still deserve to lead. At one point, I realized we weren't even fighting for control of the company. We were fighting for control of the *narrative*. Who built this. Who mattered more. Who the story would remember. That's the real sickness of success—it tricks you into thinking the win isn't real unless everyone knows it was you who won.

And that's how partnerships die—not in explosions, but in erosion. One misunderstanding at a time. One silent meeting at a time. If you think partnerships and paperwork are going to protect you, I'm here to tell you they won't. The only thing that protects you, ever, is your ability to take responsibility. That, and your ability to remember what you're building in the first place. To go all the way back to that conversation with my mom, imagine that two business partners decide to open a hospital together. What happens when they split up? What happens when neither one can be the bigger man? No more hospital, which means their "interpersonal problems" now have life or death consequences for countless others. One way or another, it's your responsibility to deal with it before someone else has to pay the price.

That's it. That's what it means to be a Rogue Visionary. Accept it or put down this book and walk away.

Still here? Good. Let's talk about rock bottom, and what it takes to climb back up from there.

Chapter 6
To the Basement (and Back Again)

You know how renters like to look at credit scores before they accept a new tenant? Yeah, mine was not so great after the collapse of SHREDZ. So, after renting out multiple penthouses through the company to house myself and all our team members, I went back to live with my parents. Actually, let me be a little more specific: I went back to live in their *basement*.

From sky high to literally underground. That was me. Or, at least, that was my living situation.

My old life sat in cardboard boxes—custom suits, brand decks, trophies from an empire that no longer existed. I stacked them along the wall like evidence of a crime I hadn't figured out how to confess to yet. My parents didn't say much. They didn't need to. Their small talk was equal parts mercy and embarrassment, both *for* me and *of* me. My mom asked if I was eating enough. My dad reminded me to move my car before the street sweeper came. That was it. Every night I'd lie awake staring at the unfinished ceiling, replaying every conversation that led to the collapse. The partners. The pride. The missed signs. I kept thinking there had to be a way to rewind it, to fix it. But there's no rewind when you've lost trust, money, and face in the same breath.

Some nights I'd grab my laptop and scroll old photos from the office—team parties, influencer shoots, a younger version of me surrounded by people who thought I could never lose. That guy looked bulletproof. That was "the prince" my parents brought to America.

Whatever I was now, I certainly wasn't that.

Still, I had bills to pay, so I turned to the one piece of advice that has both saved (and destroyed) countless entrepreneurs: when you find something that works, *double down on it*. Sounds great in theory. Such a recipe for disaster in the wrong hands.

So, before we get to my (next) disaster, let me tell you why this is *sometimes* good advice. Getting ANYTHING to work in business is a miracle. This is especially true in highly competitive, established markets. (And if you've somehow found yourself a "blue ocean" then that's its own miracle.) SHREDZ was not the first company to sell health supplements or even fat burners. Obviously. Remember, *I* was the one copying other companies' product labels at GNC back in the early days. Later, when SHREDZ was riding high, many of those same companies would try to directly copy our work with influencers.

And that's *just* competition. Let's not forget the hassles of dealing with government regulation or riding the waves of Instagram's algorithm changes. The exact problems vary by industry, but the reality does not change: *you will always have something working against you.* This means you must always have something FOR you at any given time. Is there still room for experimentation and self-expression? Yes, absolutely. In fact, those are vital components of any successful business. Still, you must never indulge those things *at the expense of* what is already working.

Yet…this is what entrepreneurs do all the time. Frankly, entrepreneurs are some of the most easily distracted people on the planet. Especially when they see all their buddies making bank off of some "killer new strategy" and want to try it for themselves. It's cute when you've got a massive operation and you can set aside a little budget and manpower for R&D. It's not cute when you gamble the entire company on an experiment that proves to be a dud.

So naturally, my first instinct was to try to do SHREDZ again under a different name. Sure, I no longer had Arvin in my corner, but what did that matter? He was the face of business. I was the one who built the bones, organs, and muscle tissue. I could do it again. I could find a new face or even build something less dependent on a single person. I just needed some seed money to get started.

Finding the seed money was relatively easy. I got a couple hundred grand from people who believed in my previous CPG success. People who looked at the nine-figure revenue run and thought, "This guy knows what he's doing." People who understood what happened behind the scenes. People who bought into the same lie I was telling myself back then. See, I had this story I kept telling myself: *The only reason SHREDZ collapsed was because of my partners. The business model was sound. The marketing was brilliant. The problem was people, not the system.* And you know what? Parts of that were true. But the conclusion I drew from those truths? Completely wrong.

I told myself I was going to start lean. Build smart. Do it right this time. What I actually did was try to recreate SHREDZ at the exact moment when everything that made SHREDZ work had fundamentally changed.

The first mistake? Payroll.

I was running an organization that once had two hundred team members, operating out of penthouses, managing thousands of influencers across multiple continents. When I needed to start over, I needed to go back to the beginning—me and a handful of people, paying them three to five grand a month, building something from scratch with hunger and hustle.

Instead, I hired people at ten, even twenty thousand dollars a month. Because that's what people were getting paid at SHREDZ. That's what the "market rate" was for talent at that level. Never mind that I was no longer operating at that level. Never mind that I didn't have the revenue infrastructure to support those salaries. I just kept spending like I was still running a nine-figure operation.

Why? Pride. Pure pride. I couldn't accept that I was starting over. I couldn't stomach the idea of calling someone I used to manage and offering them a fraction of what they used to make. So I paid them what they were "worth" and burned through investor money like it was kindling. I had victim syndrome. That's what I call it now, at least. Back then, I called it "getting screwed." I lost everything *because* of them. It had nothing to do with me. I was the guy who built the machine. They were the ones who broke it. All I needed was another shot, and I'd prove everyone wrong.

Classic victim thinking. And it's poison.

Here's the thing about victim syndrome: it feels *so good* in the moment. It lets you off the hook. It protects your ego. It gives you righteous anger to fuel your next move. But it also blinds you.

When you're convinced that external forces destroyed you, you never actually fix the internal problems that allowed those forces to win. I wasn't just burning investor money on inflated payroll. I was burning it on denial. I was trying to prove that SHREDZ could work without Arvin, without the penthouse offices, without the massive influencer network—all while refusing to acknowledge that *I* was the one who needed to change.

The companies lasted a handful of months. Maybe slightly longer. I don't even remember exactly. What I do remember is the moment I realized it was over. Not the moment I closed them down—that took longer, because I kept trying to resuscitate something that was already dead. I mean the moment I *knew*.

I was sitting at my laptop, looking at the numbers. We weren't even close. Revenue wasn't scaling. Costs were out of control. The investors were getting nervous. And I was completely out of moves. Not because I didn't know what to do—I absolutely knew what to do. I'd done it before. I just couldn't do it. Not emotionally. Not psychologically. I couldn't go back to the beginning and build something small, because doing that would mean admitting I'd lost everything.

So instead, I lost everything twice. I gave up. Shut everything down. Sent the team home. Called the investors and told them it wasn't going to work out. Some of them were understanding. Some of them weren't. I can't blame the ones who weren't.

Then I moved back into my parents' basement.

Again.

This time was different, though. Worse. The first time I moved back, I at least had the dignity of thinking it was temporary. A pit stop. A chance to regroup before the next big move. This time? I had nothing. No plan. No prospects. No energy. I was thirty-two years old, and I'd just failed at the one thing I thought I could never fail at: rebuilding.

The debt was worse now too. Way worse. The initial collapse left me with obligations from SHREDZ—personal guarantees on business loans, money I'd borrowed to try to keep things afloat. Now I had new debt on top of that. Maxed-out credit cards.

Money borrowed from friends who believed in me enough to write checks when I said I couldn't pay rent. I'd also remortgaged my parents' home. With their knowledge, of course—I'm not a complete monster. But still. They believed in me. They trusted me. They gave me power of attorney over their biggest asset, and I used it to try to save a sinking ship. All of it compounding, growing, metastasizing.

The total? $1.8 million.

My girlfriend wasn't helping. We'd been together about two years at that point. I was even thinking about proposing. But every single day, it was the same thing: "You're a failure. You should have fought harder. I can't believe you lost everything. We have nothing now."

She wasn't wrong. We *did* have nothing. But hearing it every day, in that tone, with that mix of disappointment and disgust—it hollowed me out. I hung on anyway. Because what else did I have? My friends were gone. The team members who used to wear "Team AKG" shirts? They stayed at the company after I left. They had their reasons. I don't blame them for that. But it meant I had nobody. Nobody except a girlfriend who hated me and parents who didn't know what to say.

I was a shell of the man I used to be. Not Alpha Ankur Garg anymore. Just some guy who didn't believe in himself, sitting in a basement surrounded by boxes full of proof that he used to matter.

You want to know the real kicker? The personal guarantees. When I left SHREDZ, I was still on the hook for business loans I'd signed onto during the good times. The company was supposed to handle those payments. Except now the company wasn't making those payments, which meant the lenders started calling *me*. Asking where their money was. Threatening legal action.

That's when the debt really started to compound. Not just the money I'd borrowed directly, but all the hidden obligations I'd signed my name to back when I thought nothing could go wrong. Every phone call was another few thousand added to the total. Every letter from a law firm was another creditor circling.

Again, I want to be clear about something: I made those decisions. I signed the lines with my name next to the guarantees. I took on my portion of responsibility for that debt. Nobody forced me. This wasn't some elaborate conspiracy or bad luck. It was me, making bad choices, one after another, because at the time I was too scared to bet on myself and too eager to bet on other people.

So let's talk about "doubling down on what works." Because this entire disaster is a perfect case study in how that advice can destroy you if you don't understand what it actually means.

Here's what I thought "worked" at SHREDZ:

- Inventing fitness influencer marketing
- High-quality product labels (and products, of course)
- Customized affiliate funnels and fast scaling
- Big teams with lavish perks
- Fat commission paychecks

Here's what *actually* worked at SHREDZ:

- Consistent work ethic and the trust that came with it
- A "blue ocean" moment when nobody else was doing female supplements on Instagram
- My ability to move faster than anyone else because I was hungry and had nothing to lose
- A lean, scrappy mentality that let us test and pivot instantly
- Partnership dynamics that, for a time, balanced each other out

Notice the difference? The things I thought were the "secret sauce" were actually just tactics. Tools. Methods. The things that *actually* made SHREDZ work were about context, timing, people, and mindset. You can't just copy-paste tactics from one context to another and expect them to work. But that's exactly what I tried to do.

I tried to double down on tactics without understanding the context that made them effective. I hired expensive talent without having the revenue model to support them. I tried to scale fast without the infrastructure. I tried to replicate the influencer model after Instagram had fundamentally changed how that model worked. I tried to build SHREDZ 2.0 without Arvin, without the blue ocean, without the hunger, and without the humility to admit that maybe—just maybe—I needed to start smaller.

That's the dark side of "double down on what works." If you misdiagnose *what* worked, you're not doubling down on success—you're doubling down on a fantasy. And fantasies burn money fast.

The lesson isn't "don't double down." The lesson is: be ruthlessly honest about what actually created the success you're trying to replicate. Was it the tactics? Or was it the timing, the team, the market conditions, the specific confluence of factors that will never exist again in quite the same way? Most of the time, it's one of those. Which means you can't just run the same play. You have to understand the *principles* behind why it worked, then figure out how to apply those principles in your new context.

I didn't do that. I was too busy being a victim, too busy trying to prove I was right, too busy pretending I was still the guy who built a nine-figure brand. The result? Two stints in my parents' basement. $1.8 million in debt. And a girlfriend who couldn't wait to remind me every day how badly I'd failed.

But hey, at least I learned something. Eventually.

The second time in that basement was rock bottom. Not because of the money—though that was bad—but because I finally ran out of excuses. I couldn't blame my partners anymore. I couldn't blame the lawsuits or the algorithm changes or bad luck. This failure was 100% mine. I had raised the money. I had hired the team. I had made the calls. And I had failed.

That realization didn't feel like relief. It felt like drowning. But it was also the first moment of self-honesty since leaving SHREDZ. Because once you stop lying to yourself about who's responsible, you can finally start fixing the actual problems. I wasn't ready to fix them yet. Not quite. I was still too broken, too tired, too angry at the world and at myself. But the foundation was there. The crack in the denial. The tiny seed of understanding that would eventually grow into something real.

Still, that's not an overnight process. I needed money *now*. I needed work *now*. Hell, I needed a miracle *now*. And lucky for me, I got one.

Chapter 7
The Pittsburgh Prison Sentence

Would it surprise you to hear that my girlfriend left me? Because she did. I ain't saying she was a gold digger, but I will say $1.8 million in debt has a *cooling effect* on most women.

Lucky for me, though, I still had a rich and active social life. The debt collectors would call me at all hours of the day, and there were plenty of them. They each had their own little schtick, too. Some liked to play good cop. Some liked to play bad cop. Some of them wanted to "understand my situation." Some of them said I had an awfully nice pair of kneecaps, and it would be a shame if something happened to them. Some of them even rang me from call centers and spoke with the barely concealed accents of the old country.

And, of course, I got to see my parents *every day!*

I was hanging on by a thread. I couldn't stay in that basement forever. My parents weren't going to kick me out—they loved me too much for that—but I could feel their disappointment like humidity. Thick, inescapable, making everything harder to breathe.

That's when an old friend and mentor called. Sean Marszalek, the founder and CEO of SDC Nutrition which is a manufacturing facility in Pittsburgh.

He said, "Yo I heard you're a free agent. You should come work for me."

"Sean," I told him, "There's zero chance I'm ever moving to Pittsburgh. Don't you dare try to get me to move to Pittsburgh. It's too cold."

Remember: $1.8 million in debt. Living in my parents' basement. *I did not want to move to Pittsburgh.*

"Come on," he said, "It's the same weather as Jersey. Check your email, I'm sending you a plane ticket."

I didn't believe him, but I packed anyway. When you lose everything, you stop waiting for the perfect opportunity. You just start moving—anywhere but here. Now look, I know New Jersey is not exactly paradise. But in my mind, Pittsburgh was basically Canada. Just a frozen wasteland in the distant north. When I first landed there, it confirmed all my worst fears. The bridges all looked like rib cages, the rivers moved like cold blood, and the sun—when it bothered to show—came in gray and undecided. Even the light felt like it was clocking in. Also, Pittsburgh was about 92% white. I've got nothing against white people, but I was still a Punjabi man with a beard. A *broke* Punjabi man with a beard. A Punjabi man with exactly one connection in the city. I wasn't quite sure how that was going to go down.

So at that point, I'm not even committed to the move. Sean just flew me out for a few days to talk things through. He said, "Hey man, listen, you can be my Chief Marketing Officer, and I can pay you enough money to get by, pay rent, and whatever else. Plus, I have all these other brands I manufacture for and maybe you can consult for some of them. You're okay to take on whatever side projects you want and just get out. There's nothing keeping you in Jersey anymore."

I saw his point, and ultimately agreed, but that last point wasn't exactly true. The basement wasn't rock bottom. It was the waiting room before I faced it. For all the shame of coming back home, it was still *home*. There was still half a childhood's worth of memories and all the pictures and trinkets from an extended family that spanned the globe. In Pittsburgh, I would have none of that. Honestly, I wasn't sure how I would hold up without it. I was still in such a fragile state.

Still, I knew Sean was right, so I packed up my car and drove over to Pittsburgh. I stayed in a hotel that my fraternity brother's cousin owned (I did say I was Indian right?) for the first couple of months out of sheer denial. I didn't want to say I'd "moved" to Pittsburgh, but eventually I got over myself and got a tiny little shoebox apartment in North Shore. It wasn't even that big of a stretch to call this place a "prison cell". The toilet and the kitchen were practically in the same room. It was so cheap that my *parking spot* cost more than the apartment itself. And, of course, it was in Pittsburgh. (Sorry if you're from Pittsburgh. No really, I'm sorry *for* you.)

Jokes aside, it was incredible that I even survived in that place. Or maybe it's not. Maybe it's exactly what I needed at the time. In theory, a prison cell is where you go to repent, and that's exactly what I did. I didn't party. I didn't go out. I ate the same meal every day which I managed to get for $3 from a local restaurant. It wasn't just a budget thing either—I didn't have time to cook because I was so busy working. I did every little website build or logo design I could find. I even drove Uber at night. All the kinds of things we would now call "gig work" before that was even a term. And even as bigger, juicier deals came in, I didn't stop the gig work. I just squeezed it into the cracks of my day.

Back at SHREDZ, I used to *hear* the business before I saw it— edit bays humming, email pings rolling, laughter breaking across the room like good weather. In Pittsburgh, I heard the refrigerator tick after it shut off. I could hear my own breath. Honestly, I probably heard a rat or two. Or a dozen. At night I'd scroll socials—people I had trained, people I had paid, people I had pushed into spotlights—now announcing launches, celebrating wins, taking bows. That's the real punishment no one warns you about: the success you helped architect, humming along just fine without you. I told myself the silence was productive. That solitude was strategy. And ultimately, I was right.

In six months, I paid off all my debt. All $1.8 million. You want a 7-figure *annual* income? I got myself to 7 figures in 6 months. And by "myself" I mean all my creditors. Still, I built it, and this time with way less going for me than ever before. If you don't think it's possible for you to hit that level of *income* then, frankly, you might just be too comfortable. People think rebuilding is all momentum and late-night epiphanies. Sometimes it's just showing up to a quiet room and choosing not to leave or find a distraction. Sometimes it's the discipline of not filling the silence with the wrong noise—no new partnerships to cover your ass, no reckless hires to cosplay confidence, no victory posts for a war you haven't won. No bottles. No girls. No glamour.

The city didn't care who I used to be. That was the gift. Pittsburgh kept its head down and dared me to match it.

Still, it was hard to take too much pride in that particular milestone. I had barely celebrated my first million, now I was supposed to celebrate…what, exactly? Clawing my way *back up to zero?* And it's not like servicing the debt magically fixed all my other problems.

Losing money is arithmetic. You can count it. You can refill it, no matter how deep the hole is. Losing identity is geometry. Suddenly there are angles you never knew your life had. Every memory bends. Every story tilts. You look back at your "wins" and wonder if they were just better-lit losses. What if I'd left earlier? What if I'd pushed harder? What if I'd just bowed down to Arvin's will so I could stay at the company?

Here's a truth I wish more founders said out loud: there are nights when the idea of not waking up feels like a relief. But since I kept waking up and kept breathing, and I had no plans to change that myself, I had to figure out my plan for the future. I almost *missed* the debt once I'd paid it off. That was at least a clear, achievable goal. Once it was gone, I had to figure out, "What do I do with *this* money?"

That's when I had to confront the reality lurking behind all of this: I no longer believed in myself. I *knew* that I could *do* good work, but I wasn't holding my head high. I needed more than just the numbers. I needed to feel like a real man again. And in the weirdest way, that's when life threw me a left hook.

Sean and I were grabbing coffee one morning when a couple at a table nearby *detonated*. Not cute bickering. Full-volume, public, why-are-we-all-here-for-this arguing. He storms out. She starts crying. I should probably mention that she was really hot too. Not that matters. I would've totally been a gentleman either way. Promise. So I grabbed a glass of water and walked over.

"Hey. That dude's an asshole. Everything will be okay."

She shook her head. "That's not my man."

Now I'm confused. "Okay… then why the tears?"

She tells me about this big Pittsburgh nonprofit competition she's helping to run. Everyone chooses a cause, raises money, gets judged. Her category? A charity boxing event. Amateur fighters with trainers, real ring, real crowd. That dude was one of her boxers, and he just quit. The event was three weeks away.

"Where am I going to find another boxer?"

Before my brain could stop my mouth, I heard myself say, "I can't box, but I'll do it."

"Seriously? There's no way you can be trained in time," she said.

So, I'm like, "Listen, I will do whatever it takes to get you to stop crying right now."

And that's how I started living out my own version of *Rocky*. Every morning I'd get up at 3:00 a.m., go straight to the gym, and do whatever the trainer told me. When we first started, I weighed in at 285lbs and it was painfully obvious I wouldn't stand a chance in the ring. Lucky for me, though, the fight got pushed back two months. With three months of training, I got down to 215. I was lean and looking good.

Of course, if you've ever actually *seen the first Rocky movie* then you know how this ends. I lost the fight. Actually, I didn't even really lose. I tripped on the mat in the middle of the second round and then they called the fight. I guess they didn't want to risk Punjabi Pooh-Bear getting ripped to shreds at a charity event.

Still, the whole experience jumpstarted my confidence in just the way I needed. I was finally able to put myself out there on camera like I did back in Jersey. I got on YouTube and started taking my social media presence seriously again. That, in turn, opened up all kinds of new opportunities that I couldn't just hustle my way into the old-fashioned way.

For the record, nothing ever happened between that girl and me romantically. Instead, we became friends and I ended up introducing her to her now husband. Honestly, Pittsburgh girls were never really my type. For one, 92% of them were white, like I mentioned before, and I think for a lot of them I was the closest thing they could find to a black guy. So, I fell into this weird pattern where we'd match and hit it off on dating apps, but they'd never show up for the actual dates. For two, Pittsburg girls get in your face. Jersey girls talk back to you. That might seem like a minor distinction, but trust me, it changes everything. That's part of why I'm now happily married to a Jersey girl.

Anyway, the point is I got my swagger back. I even got back my full mustache! Remember when I said the alopecia caused half of it to disappear? Now, with all this newfound confidence working its way through my body, all those hairs came back. And between that and all the momentum I'd built up in business, this is when I truly became a Rogue Visionary.

No, literally. Around this same time, a brand brought me in to consult on their marketing. Their decks were clean, their metrics were mush, and their ad creative looked like someone exported a PowerPoint. I told them the truth: they were burning $60,000 a month on ads that looked like homework. No hook. No psychology. No reason for anyone to stop scrolling other than pity.

Silence. A throat clear. Then some suited-up little penguin across the table tilted his head and smirked.

"You're kind of a rogue visionary, huh?"

That's right. The title of this book started as an insult. It dribbled out of the mouth of someone who is *not* a Rogue Visionary. Someone who hadn't seen a tenth of what I've seen and probably still hasn't. So I just nodded. Because I knew what they really meant: You're unpredictable. You challenge things we've accepted for too long. You make us uncomfortable.

Good.

I told you being a Rogue Visionary is not some cute little title. You don't get hired to nod politely. You get hired because you say the thing no one else will. Because you care more about results than your reputation. The truth is, most people use "visionary" as a polite way to say, "delusional until it works." And they say "rogue" for someone they consider a threat.

But you know what I've learned? All the people who ever made anything worth remembering started off rogue. They didn't ask for consensus. They didn't wait for the industry to catch up. They didn't explain themselves to people who didn't have the range. They just built.

That's what I did. That's what every Rogue Visionary does. And like any other title, even the ones that start out as insults, it's *given*, not chosen. It means you've lost before. It means you've bet on yourself when it would've been easier to play small. It means you've stayed up until 3 a.m. rethinking your entire client strategy—not because you had to, but because you couldn't not.

And no, it doesn't come easy. You lose clients who want safety. You outgrow partners who can't keep up. You get labeled "difficult," "intense," "too much." But if you're building something real, you should be too much for most. That's the cost of clarity in a world addicted to compromise. So when they call you Rogue? Say thank you. When they say you're Visionary then chuckle as you leave the room? Hold your head high.

It means they finally noticed what you've been doing in silence.

Chapter 8
The Five MBAs (None from Harvard)

I realize I barely talked about my time at SDC Nutrition in the last chapter. I guess Pittsburgh was more of a treasure trove than I gave it credit for.

SDC Nutrition wasn't a startup. It wasn't a hustle. It was a *manufacturing facility*—the kind of place where processes matter, where SOPs aren't optional, and where cutting corners means contaminated product batches and FDA violations. Sean knew what he was doing when he brought me in as Chief Marketing Officer. He wasn't just giving me a title. He was forcing me to learn how real companies operate when they're not held together by duct tape and caffeine.

For three years, I lived inside that world. I learned how to document workflows. How to create repeatable systems that didn't depend on one person's genius or hustle. How to scale operations without breaking them. This was the opposite of everything I'd built in Jersey—and that was exactly the point. At SHREDZ, I *was* the system. If something really needed to get done, I did it. If a problem arose, I fixed it. Those little SOPs I wrote back then were *adorable*, and they did nothing to protect anyone when shit hit the fan.

At SDC, I couldn't be the bottleneck. Nobody could be, even if they were in the C Suite. The operation was too complex, the stakes too high. I had to build frameworks that worked without me. I had to trust other people to execute. And I had to accept that boring, methodical, process-driven work was just as valuable as the flashy creative stuff I'd always chased. Best of all, I was surrounded by systems already built like that.

There's a certain kind of entrepreneur who loves to talk trash about Corporate America. Who loves to beat his chest about "freedom" and being a "rebel" because he never went into Corporate America or got out early. Let me be crystal clear: this is not how Rogue Visionaries think. The drawbacks of Corporate America are real, as we'll get into in a moment. Still, I have nothing but respect for the people who build these systems and the people who work within them. It takes ungodly amounts of discipline, forward thinking, and attention to detail to keep these systems running. And, on the tail end of it all are *millions of happy customers!* That's the only way you CAN create such a massive operation. So no, I don't think anyone deserves bragging rights just because they operate outside of Corporate America. How about you LEARN from Corporate America, use that knowledge to make your thing bulletproof, and then you can brag.

Like I mentioned before, Sean also gave me permission to consult for the other brands SDC manufactured for. That opened a whole new revenue stream and a whole new set of lessons. These weren't my brands. I didn't have equity. I didn't have control. But I *did* have expertise, and I learned how to package that expertise in ways that made sense to founders who didn't know what they didn't know. That guy who made the "Rogue Visionary" comment in the last chapter? That was during one of these meetings.

I also started co-hosting a podcast with Sean called *We Make Supplements*. The premise was simple: pull back the curtain on the supplement industry. Show people how products actually get made, what regulations exist, where brands cut corners, and how to avoid the common pitfalls that sink most supplement startups. It was part education, part entertainment, part therapy for me. Talking through the mistakes I'd made at SHREDZ in a structured, public way forced me to process them differently. I wasn't just surviving anymore. I was synthesizing.

Still, Pittsburgh had its limits. The debt was gone. The confidence was back. But I was still living in that shoebox apartment, still grinding 80-hour weeks, still feeling like I was treading water instead of swimming forward. I needed something bigger. Something that would prove I could succeed in a context that had nothing to do with supplements or influencers or Jersey Shore.

That's when COVID caused my close friends at SDC to make a decision to bench the marketing division out of uncertainty of what was going to happen next...

I had to start over again, but I wasn't going to rebuild from my parent's basement. Instead, I found a way to stay in Pittsburgh until the right opportunity found me.

That's when biotech found me.

It started with a favor for an old friend. His wife worked at a stem cell-based biotech company—legitimate, clinical trials, placental stem cell banking, and more—and they needed a new website. I said yes because that's what I do. I build websites. I solve problems. I show up. When I delivered the site within 48 hours, the CEO called me and asked me to drop everything to come meet with him.

So naturally, I asked myself, "Who the heck does he think he is?" and I decided to Google him. Let's just say his name was on the same playing field as Elon Musk. So I drove over to Jersey, took a shower at my parents', put on a suit, and drove over to their office. Within 30 seconds he asked the same question Arvin had asked me years earlier: "What else can you do?"

I smiled. "Everything. What do you need me to do?"

They needed storytelling, marketing, and branding. They were on the verge of a SPAC merger—basically going public through a backdoor deal—and they had *zero* marketing infrastructure. No messaging. No campaigns. No clear go-to-market strategy. Just a lot of smart scientists who knew how to make pharmaceutical products but had no idea how to sell them.

I joined as the lead of the marketing team. Not as a consultant this time, but as an actual employee. W-2. Benefits. The whole thing. For the first time in my life, I was working IN corporate. Real corporate. The kind with org charts and quarterly reviews and senior leadership who cared about your pedigree as much as your performance.

It was culture shock.

At SHREDZ, nobody cared where you went to school. They cared if you could execute. If you moved fast, stayed hungry, and produced results, you belonged. In biotech? It was the opposite. The first time I walked into a strategy meeting, I noticed the dynamic immediately. The executives with Harvard and Stanford degrees got deference. Their ideas were treated like gospel. The rest of us—Rutgers, state schools, "no-name" universities—had to fight for every inch of credibility.

I hated it. But I also understood it. Biotech isn't supplements. You can't just slap a pink label on a product and hope for the best. Clinical trials. FDA approvals. Pharmaceutical-grade manufacturing standards. These are high-stakes, high-complexity environments where one mistake can kill people or end a company. The people running these operations needed to trust that you knew what you were doing, and pedigree was their shortcut to trust.

Still, pedigree prejudice is real. I'd walk into rooms where my ideas were dismissed until someone from an Ivy League school said the same thing five minutes later. Then suddenly it was brilliant. I learned to navigate that dynamic the way I'd learned to navigate everything else: by producing undeniable results. You can question my degree. You can't question the campaign that just drove a 40% lift in lead generation.

What shocked me most about corporate life wasn't the politics or the hierarchy. It was the *schedule*. For the first time in my adult life, I worked 9-to-5. I came home at normal hours. I had evenings. I had weekends off. I didn't collapse into bed at 2 a.m. after an eighteen-hour shift. I just...worked. Like a normal person.

It felt wrong at first. Like I was slacking. But then I realized: this is what sustainable business looks like. You don't have to kill yourself to be effective. You just have to have the right systems in place. That was Sean's lesson, refined. Structure doesn't limit you. It *frees* you. Even when I took work home with me (which I often did) it felt different. It wasn't an expectation. It was my choice. I *wanted* to be excellent, so I still went after it even when the ball was in my court.

I also started reading management books for the first time. Not because I wanted to, but because I had to. In biotech, you didn't just wing it. You needed frameworks. Mental models. Proven approaches to leadership, communication, and decision-making. I devoured books on corporate strategy, organizational behavior, and change management. I learned the language of executives. I learned how to translate my entrepreneurial instincts into something that made sense in boardrooms. It was very different from the chaos of clubs and penthouses and herding influencers like cats. And for a while, I thought maybe this was the answer. Maybe I'd been doing it wrong the whole time. Maybe the key to success wasn't hustle and instinct—it was structure and strategy. Maybe I was finally growing up.

Then November 2022 hit.

The money in biotech dried up. Funding evaporated. Investors pulled back. The SPAC deal that was supposed to change everything? It fell short of expectations. And when biotech companies lose funding, they don't cut incrementally. They cut *deep*.

Ninety percent of the staff got an infamous "warning letter" aka you're getting laid off. Yeah, even I was on the list.

Marketing is always first to go. That's a rule I've learned the hard way, again and again. When the money runs out, companies cut the "soft" functions first. Sales, maybe you keep. Operations, definitely. But marketing? That's a luxury. A nice-to-have. Not mission-critical.

I was thirty-seven years old, starting over for the fifth time. I sat in my car after getting the news and just stared at the steering wheel. I didn't cry. I didn't rage. I just thought, *here we go again.* But this time, something was different. I wasn't spiraling. I wasn't panicking. I wasn't drowning in shame or victim mentality. I was just...processing. Because by then, I'd done this enough times to recognize the pattern. Lose everything. Rebuild. Learn. Repeat.

This wasn't failure anymore. It was data.

Before the biotech layoff, I'd already made another move. COVID hit in 2020, and suddenly the world shut down. Pittsburgh was manageable when I could travel, when I could visit friends and family on weekends, when I had some semblance of a social life. But locked down in that shoebox apartment? It was unbearable.

More than that, I was worried about my parents. They were in New Jersey, and they were getting up there in age. Never mind that people were getting *weird* around COVID, and they lived right in the city where the restrictions were tight, and the crazies couldn't care less.

I called them one night and said, "I'm coming home. I don't want you guys to be alone for all this."

They protested. They didn't want me to uproot my life again. But I was done with Pittsburgh anyway. Sean and I had accomplished what we set out to do. I'd paid off my debt. I'd rebuilt my confidence. I'd learned how real operations worked. It was time to move on. So, in late 2019, I packed up and headed back to Jersey. Again. For the fourth time. Or fifth, depending on how you count.

But this time, I wasn't moving back to the basement. I got my own place—a nice apartment in Jersey City. I was consulting. I was building. I even bought a car for the first time in my life. Best of all, I found a nice Jersey girl and got engaged. For the first time in years, my life felt *normal*. Not perfect. Not flashy. Just stable.

Then biotech ended, and I was back to square one. Except I wasn't. Not really.

Here's what I realized after the fifth restart: I had five MBAs. Not formal ones. Not from Harvard or Wharton or any of the schools that would've given me automatic credibility in corporate boardrooms. But real-world MBAs. The kind you earn by failing, rebuilding, and paying attention to what went wrong.

The first MBA was SHREDZ. I learned how to build a brand from nothing, how to pioneer a new marketing channel, how to scale fast, and how to lose everything when partnerships go toxic.

The second MBA was the post-SHREDZ startups. I learned what happens when you try to recreate past success without understanding the context that made it work. I learned about victim mentality and how it poisons decision-making.

The third MBA was Pittsburgh. I learned structure, systems, and operational discipline. I learned how to document processes and build businesses that don't depend on one person's heroics.

The fourth MBA was biotech. I learned corporate politics, pedigree dynamics, and how to translate entrepreneurial instincts into language that resonates in high-stakes, regulated environments.

The fifth MBA was the layoffs. I learned that no job is safe, no industry is immune, and the only real security is the ability to rebuild faster than circumstances can tear you down.

Each failure built specific expertise. Each restart taught me something I couldn't have learned any other way. And by the time I hit thirty-eight, I wasn't running from the pattern anymore. I was understanding it.

I know how to build and create and grow in any format I want. I know what works in scrappy startups and what works in structured corporations. I know how to launch products, manage teams, navigate regulations, and pivot when markets shift. I know all the ways things can go wrong because I've lived through most of them.

And here's the thing: I'm not angry about it anymore. I'm not embarrassed. I'm not a victim. I'm a student. Every scar is a lesson. Every collapse is data. Every restart is proof that I can survive anything. By the time I moved back to Jersey for good, I was ready for what came next. Not because I had all the answers, but because I'd finally stopped pretending, I needed them. I just needed to trust myself, build the right partnerships, and keep moving.

Now, does that mean all my problems were solved? *Absolutely not.* I had a big fat Indian wedding to plan, and pay for, without the biotech dollars I'd been planning on. So, I had to dig deep. I had to find the juice to rebuild AGAIN and make it stick this time. And that's when I found myself tapping back into maybe the most important part of my upbringing. The one thing I purposely omitted because it's taken me a lifetime to understand its true power.

Chapter 9
My Third Parent

Way back in Chapter 2, I told you how my parents worked around the clock to create better opportunities for us. I told you they would send me out to my aunt in Delaware for the summers. I told you how, by the time I got to high school, I was keeping myself plenty busy with schoolwork, DJing, and…let's call them "early forays into pharmaceuticals".

But if you stop and do the math there, that leaves a lot of time where I was left unattended. Time where I was just a lonely, only child whiling away the hours in our tiny New Jersey apartment. That gap is where my secret third parent stepped in. My third parent who, in the most critical parts of my life, saved me from myself.

I'm talking about 90s television.

Family Matters taught me about loyalty and family bonds that went beyond blood. Watching Carl Winslow defend his kids when they were arrested for being Black, seeing him walk into that police station and scare the living hell out of those officers to get his kids released—that was power. That was the kind of power I wanted. Not violence. Not aggression. Just the ability to walk into a room and command respect through sheer presence.

Now Will Smith from *The Fresh Prince*, he showed me something entirely different about who I wanted to be. This character was the guy who could charm his way through anything, but Uncle Phil was the one who taught him—and me—about responsibility. That scene where Will's father leaves him again, and Uncle Phil just holds him while he breaks down? That hit different. It taught me that strength wasn't about never showing weakness. It was about being there when someone else was weak.

But it was *Saved by the Bell* that became my real education. I didn't want to be AC Slater. I didn't want to be Screech. I wanted to be Zack Morris. This dude had Kelly Kapowski—the girl everyone wanted—but it wasn't because he was the strongest or the smartest or the richest. It was because he knew how to read people. He knew how to make people feel like they mattered. Ultimately, he knew how to bend reality itself.

I remember this one episode where Zack crashes his car—completely wrecks it—and he's supposed to be in massive trouble. But instead of panicking, he orchestrates this whole thing where his friends help him stage the situation so perfectly that he basically gets away with it. No screaming. No begging. Just strategic thinking and the ability to convince people to do what he needed them to do. Another time, he needed to get all his female friends to pose for a bikini calendar so he could raise money. Did he beg? Did he bribe them? Nah. He made it sound like the most natural, fun thing in the world. He made them *want* to do it. That's persuasion at its finest.

I sat day after day and watched every episode like it was a masterclass. I started noticing the patterns. Zack would assess what the other person wanted, then he'd position his request as the solution to their problem. He'd use humor to disarm people. He'd create urgency when he needed to. He'd know when to push and when to back off.

But here's what really got me: Zack wasn't a manipulator in the toxic sense. He genuinely cared about his friends. He just also happened to be really good at getting people to see things his way. That's what I wanted to master. Not the ability to con people, but the ability to align interests so everyone wins.

I started applying these lessons everywhere. Whenever I'd see something, I wanted—a Linkin Park CD, the new Nintendo game, a pair of sneakers that didn't look like they came off the clearance rack—and I'd ask. And my parents would say no. Not because they didn't love me. Not because they were trying to deprive me. But because they were financially responsible. They were playing the long game. They were holding the line, and on some level I already understood that.

So, then I thought, "All right, who else has the money? And how can I align our interests, so they give it to me?"

I picked up a paper route before most kids even had alarm clocks. I started tutoring neighborhood kids—math, reading, literally, whatever I could teach. I got into DJing and learned how to throw parties—*real* ones. In New Jersey, no less. I rented out halls, partnered with kids from other schools, figured out logistics, booked gear, made flyers. Charged admission. Even got a cut from the juice and soda bar.

At every turn, I was fashioning myself into the "Indian Zack Morris". The guy who could get anything he wanted *because* everyone else loved him and wanted to be around him. The guy who was absolutely fearless because he knew he could bounce back from any mistake. The guy who could literally bend reality.

Crucially, it wasn't just Zack's people skills that allowed him to do all this. *It was his belief in himself.* And he wasn't the only one. You could see the same thing with Will Smith in *The Fresh Prince of Bel Air*. Or even Steve Urkel from *Family Matters* when he transformed into Stefan Urquelle. Really, 90s TV was full of these larger-than-life characters driven by unwavering self-belief. Was it always realistic? *No, of course not!* That wasn't the point. The point was that these characters taught young people like me to believe in ourselves to the same degree.

Case in point, in high school I started reading everything I could get my hands on about influence and persuasion. I read *How to Win Friends and Influence People* by Dale Carnegie, which by that point just felt like review. In fact, most of those "grown up" books did. The only one that really stuck out to me was *The Art of Woo* by Mario Moussa, G. Richard Shell. The book is full of stories about how historical figures convinced people to do extraordinary things. Napoleon convincing his army to fight when they were surrounded by five enemy forces. Sam Walton being convinced to name his convenience store "Walmart" through persuasive language. The whole book is about understanding that you can rewrite reality if you can tell a good story.

Later on I learned that there are "love languages"—ways that different people prefer to receive affection. I learned that there are also respect languages and loyalty languages too. Some people feel respected when you acknowledge their time. Others feel respected when you ask for their advice. Some people feel loved through acts of service. Others need words of affirmation. I also got deep into the Myers Briggs personality types and even got StrengthsFinder certified.

With each new book I read or certification I completed, I picked up another little framework or "fun fact" to spice up a conversation. Still, the more I studied, the more I realized that everything I needed to know about business I'd learned from watching Zack Morris convince Mr. Belding to let him carry out another scheme. The confidence. The creativity. The ability to turn a "no" into a "maybe" and a "maybe" into a "yes." So when people ask me where I learned to sell, where I learned to lead, where I learned to build brands, I tell them the truth: I learned it from my third parent. I learned it from a TV character who taught me that the most powerful tool you have isn't money or connections or even talent. It's the ability to make people believe in your vision…and the ability to believe in yourself.

Now I need you to understand something here. I know it might sound a little too cute to talk about how much 90s TV still influences me as an adult. But it does, and it saved my life. Literally.

March of 2023 was not a good time for me. When I say I was in the middle of planning my "big fat Indian wedding" that is actually a huge understatement. Weddings are serious in India. It's not just the union of the bride and groom; it's the union of two *families.* There is immense pressure on both sides to show off what *kind* of family you are. That is why the wedding needs to be an event (really, a series of events) and those events cost MONEY.

My money had just fallen into the biotech black hole. I was in the middle of starting my life over, once again, for the fourth or fifth time. It would have been bad enough if I was still single. Now I had two families to let down. Now I had a woman I loved, a woman who was ready to stay by my side through thick and thin, and things were getting *really* thin. And in case that wasn't enough to test her, I was about to test the relationship even further.

I was out at an EXPO in East Rutherford, NJ, scrambling to make things happen, when I got a DUI.

Now…let's be clear about what happened there. I wasn't just "a little over the limit". I was *obliterated*, and I got behind the wheel. As a 37-year-old man, not as some dumb teenager. Looking back, it is painfully obvious to me what was going on. You don't drink like that if you still want to be here. At that point, a part of me didn't. But you know which part of me *did* want to be here? You know which part of me still thought I could make it?

The Indian Zack Morris. That rowdy inner teenager that refused to accept defeat or take "no" for an answer. That shameless life of the party that knew he could wrap up any crisis in a neat 30-minute block (with time for commercials too). I know that's not "rational" but the other part of me was even less rational. Sure, I was on the 4th or 5th restart of my life and career, but you want to hear a crazy statistic? The average millionaire has gone completely broke *three times* before finally getting their wealth to stick. Key word: average. I know absurdly wealthy people who have gone way over that number. Sometimes *by choice!*

So no, it's never "rational" to accept defeat. And whatever you need to hold onto to stay here and keep fighting, *use it.* For me it was 90s television. For you it could be your Labubu collection or your hope the New York Jets will someday return to the Super Bowl. Or it could be something even more insane (if that's even possible).

Even though I was subconsciously trying to escape, I hung in there. Sure, it was awkward at first. I went through a few months of avoiding people afterwards. But ultimately, I cleaned up my mess and did what I had to do to earn my wife's trust back, including a stint in in-patient rehab. We made it through the wedding planning and the wedding itself. She is my wife now, and I wouldn't want to be with anyone else. Somehow, even after all this, she still feels the same way.

That same night, I had another full circle moment that, ultimately, helped pull me back from the brink. See, in between all those reruns of *Saved by the Bell*, I would see commercials for all kinds of products with a big, red "As Seen on TV" logo slapped on the box. That logo was created by Ajit "A. J." Khubani, also known as the "Infomercial King". Like me, his family immigrated from India to New Jersey to find better opportunities. Unlike me, he was born back in 1959, on American soil. His firm Telebrands (now BulbHead) was and still is a sprawling commercial empire. While I was at the expo, I met his nephew, Rishi Khubani.

Like me, Rishi was going through a rough patch. He had just had a string of losses and was now the black sheep of the family. I could relate, of course. So, we hit it off that night and stayed in touch afterwards. As our friendship grew, we both wound up coaching each other in different ways. He was born into an empire; I was still struggling to build mine. I could give him a better understanding of his family's past, and the grit it takes to make the climb. He could give me his raw, honest perspective on life "up on the mountaintop". Together, we were able to extract the wisdom from our scars and rediscover our gratitude for everything we had.

And with that little reminder of *who I am*, I was ready to buckle down and build my best thing yet.

Chapter 10
AKG Creative, Reborn as an Empire

On paper, AKG Creative existed as early as 2006. But *this* version of AKG Creative did not.

Care to guess how I came up with the name? Yep, it's my own initials plus "Creative". It's a fine starting point, and it's something I see up and coming entrepreneurs do all the time. There's even a part of it I respect. By putting your own name on something, you're saying, "I am responsible for this". As we've seen throughout my story so far, that's essential. Still, it *can* speak to a certain lack of clarity. Telling the world your own name doesn't really establish what you *do* or *who* it's for, which are the core questions at heart of any major brand.

Case in point, up until 2023 AKG Creative was simply a catch-all for my different marketing ventures. Whether I was designing logos, building websites, or "consulting" in all the different forms that it takes, it all fell under AKG Creative. The thing is, though, that's not how you build an empire. Nobody's going to come along and hand you a bucket of empire-shaped puzzle pieces to put together at your leisure. Instead, you need to have a vision. You need to understand what massive problem you're solving in the marketplace, and you need to have your own unique solution. Otherwise, quite frankly, you're just taking orders and you're bound to get paid accordingly.

My vision came together over the course of 2023. When I finally sat down to review everything I'd been through, I started to see a pattern. 2023 was a very different landscape than 2011, when we first launched SHREDZ. No, I couldn't just go back and do what we did then. I already tried that, remember? Besides, the Internet had gotten so much wider in the intervening decade. Sure, Facebook and Instagram were still around, and even Snapchat was floating around somewhere, but now Twitter was turning into X and YouTube was suddenly the world's 2nd biggest search engine behind its owner, Google. Famous podcasters had been a key component of major political campaigns, and the entire ecosystem was getting rocked by the 800-pound Chinese gorilla named TikTok.

In so many ways, the Internet of 2023 was more chaotic than the Internet of 2011. More divided. More skeptical. More hostile. More centralized but weirdly more siloed at the same time. Unlike in 2011, I knew we couldn't just rely on one magic platform with one killer strategy. Not unless we wanted to run ourselves to death on someone else's hamster wheel. So instead, I zoomed out. I started looking at how content travels *across* platforms…and that's when it hit me.

The future was in podcasts. But not just any podcast. We were already well past the early days of podcasting, when you could pull a couple of your buddies together on Zoom, record yourselves shooting the breeze, and hope for the best. You needed more strategy than that. You needed a podcast built around a core message that was broad enough to come through in an elevator pitch, but also wide enough to attract a variety of guest stars and their followers. In fact, you couldn't *just* think of it as a podcast. You had to think of it as the tip of the spear for an entire media empire. You needed not just audio, but video so you could put the podcast up on YouTube as well. You needed hosts and guests alike who were prepared to chat casually but still find a way to work in core talking points throughout the conversation, so that those clips could be pulled out for TikTok, Instagram Reels, and YouTube Shorts.

In other words, you needed to launch with a clear BRAND from day one, episode one.

That's exactly what I started working on. I already knew I could build brands like nobody's business. I'd just been so busy building them for other people I'd hardly built my own. So my next big move for AKG Creative was to create my own podcast studio. And in classic Zack Morris fashion, I did it by finding someone else who already had one and making sure our interests aligned. My friend Kaushal Majmudar already owned a coworking space in town called FlexworkNJ, so I partnered with him to create Flexwork Studios. I got to skip the expense and hassle of building out a new studio and he got a steady stream of premium clients, since you can charge a lot more for a recording space than you can for a typical coworking desk.

One of the first times it clicked was with Logan Fields.

Logan didn't walk in with a polished brand, a killer studio, or some massive budget. What he had was an incredible track record of building apps for Fortune 500 companies and even NASA. All this from a guy who used to be a pastor and got paid in free ice cream to build his first app from a local creamery. He even named his company "The App Guys" because…well, that's what they are. When we first met, he was literally recording voice memos on his phone and calling it a podcast. No mic. No visuals. No clue how to build traction.

But that's what made him the perfect guinea pig.

We took Logan's raw recordings and turned them into a fully fleshed-out show. Not just episodes, but intros, trailers, thumbnails, and reels. Each piece was intentional. Each episode wasn't just posted—it was positioned. And then it happened: his DMs started lighting up. Not with vanity likes or empty praise, but with CEO's ready to get started with custom apps. Plus, he kept getting questions like, "Who does your content?" and "Can they help me too?"

Logan and others became the first proof of concept. That signal that Flexwork Studios wasn't just a cool idea—it was the beginning of something real.

That's when I realized: we weren't just building one media empire. We were building the blueprint for others to follow. So we created clear tiers for podcasters at every level—whether they just wanted a room and a camera, or they wanted us to produce, publish, and even monetize the entire thing for them. We called it:

- **No Frills** (just the studio space),
- **Be My Producer** (we do the heavy lifting), and
- **Market + Manage + Monetize** (the full engine).

My goal, of course, was to land those "whale clients" who could justify the full engine. Still, I knew better than anyone that tomorrow's empire builder is today's hustler. I wanted to be the guy who could take them all the way to the top, no matter where they are starting.

Speaking on monetization, that was another thing that made us unique (and still does). While most podcasters get into the game with vague hopes of landing sponsorships, the reality is that traditional sponsorships are only getting more and more competitive every year. Not only does this make it harder for the average podcaster to land a sponsorship, it means that sponsorship will likely pay out way less than it did in the old days. So instead, we decided to help our podcasters monetize in one of two ways (or even both). Option 1: be like Logan and sell a high-ticket service on the backend. The App Guys aren't cheap, nor should they be given the quality of the apps they deliver, so Logan's not chasing sponsorship dollars: he's buying mindshare in the eyes of his ideal clients. Or option 2: Sell your own consumer product OR sell a consumer product from one of the many brands I already own or partner with under the AKG umbrella.

Remember: I never gave up the consumer products arm of the business. The only difference is now; I either create my own brands in-house or find promising start ups and work out an equity deal with them. So, if you come to me, as an aspiring podcaster, with a burning message but no clue how to monetize it? No problem. I can point you to the right sponsors or BE the right sponsor, and I can get you a way better deal than you're ever going to find wandering in the podcast wilderness.

In other words, this is when AKG Creative stopped being a freelancer's shop and became a true holding company. For example, Grill Party BBQ was a brand we created and used as our test kitchen for brand incubation. New product ideas, seasonal drops, and high-octane visual storytelling all lived there. It taught us how to build CPG brands from scratch—fast. Then came the scale clients like Bang Cookies, CollagenFit, Saheer Wellness, and Ammave. In those cases, the founders approached us, then we designed the brands. We built the websites. We ran the ads. We owned the growth—and in some cases, we even owned equity.

Finally, the math shifted in 2024. It didn't happen overnight. There was no magical deal, no celebrity co-sign. What did happen was *stacking*—the compounding effect of consistent wins across every entity we controlled. Between monthly retainers from our CPG clients, podcast studio packages (booked out months in advance), brand incubations with equity upside, and fractional CMO deals, we crossed the $1 million mark, and we were on our way.

And that created its own problems.

See, once you hit that mid-tier growth stage, the noise creeps in. Advisors start giving conflicting advice. Your peers either can't relate or won't be honest. And worst of all—you start second-guessing yourself, not because you're wrong, but because you're *tired.* Right up until this point, I was convinced it would be different this time. That building to this point without a major business partner like Arvin would give me greater clarity and peace of mind. Instead, it only left me feeling more isolated. It only left me more desperate for a mentor or even just a companion.

I looked around and thought, "Where's the room for people like me?" I searched for a mentor. Sent the emails. Took the coffee meetings. Paid for masterminds. And I kept hearing the same thing:

"You're doing great!"

That's not mentorship. That's applause. And I wasn't interested in a standing ovation. I wanted someone who could fill in my blind spots. I wanted someone who could help me see around corners. I wanted someone to look me in the eye and *challenge* me.

But no one was ahead of me on the exact road I was on. Because I wasn't walking a road—I was building one. That was the hardest part to accept: there was no blueprint for what I was doing. So I stopped looking for one. I started trusting my own instincts again. And when I did? Everything got clearer.

I changed how I hired. Changed how I scoped work. Stopped working with clients who didn't respect the seat I'd earned. And I made mistakes—*a lot* of them. Costly ones. Emotional ones. Tactical ones. But they were mine. And they became part of the internal compass I couldn't buy, borrow, or download.

Now listen carefully because this is the part a lot of entrepreneurs don't understand: *I'm not saying I did everything myself*. Far from it. I'm saying I *owned* every part of the process. That is an absolutely essential distinction, both on paper and in your mind. There's no such thing as "independence" when you're building an empire. Everything comes down to "inter-dependence", meaning both sides can depend on each other. That is the only way you build systems like this at scale, like I learned back when I was working corporate. But, like I learned in my early days as a hustler, instinct counts too. In fact, you need to learn how to harness not just *your* instincts, but *other people's* instincts as well.

At SHREDZ we did this by bringing on influencers as affiliates. They had their custom websites to prove the sale belonged to them, we sent them a "boom" whenever they got paid, and that was it. Sure, we paid attention to the influencer space to stay on top of trends, but outside of that it wasn't very collaborative. Thus, when push came to shove, it devolved into a popularity contest, and they all chose Arvin because he was the one they could relate to. It wasn't really an empire at all. It was a mercenary band with a tiny corps of dedicated soldiers working in the penthouse. I made the mistake of putting my financial future in Arvin's hands, but really, the whole company had put its future in the hands of those influencers.

AKG Creative does not work like that. Here, I'm building a network where everybody *gets* something, and everybody *gives* something. None of it works without the other interlocking parts. People at every level—team members, vendors, partners who share equity—they're all happy to participate because it serves their needs. *They also understand it would be very, very difficult to replace all of this.* That is how it has to be, if you're going to build an empire.

Of course, at the core of any empire is a trusted circle of advisors and generals. Though I maintain a majority stake in the company, there are the select few who *do* have their own piece of equity. They get to have it because they each have their own unique superpowers, and because I want them to be directly incentivized to grow the business.

So, let's talk about who they are, what their superpowers are, and why I chose them to be in my circle.

Chapter 11
Assembling My Avengers

Deep down, I believe everyone has a superpower. The hard part is figuring out how to find it, harness it, and ultimately own it. The people who can do all three? Those are the people who literally shape the world. Your Walt Disney's, of course, but even the people behind the scenes who orchestrate those operations at scale. So, in my mind, the difference between an A-player and a B-player or even a C-player is *not* natural ability. It's how much they've taken ownership of their natural abilities.

One of my superpowers is to find those people and help them make that leap.

Case in point, Ludwig Araujo and I go back to the SHREDZ days. He was actually working as Arvin's supervisor at Verizon when Arvin left to join me full-time at SHREDZ. At the time, Ludwig was stuck in that corporate quicksand where your title doesn't change, your paycheck doesn't grow, and your soul slowly dies one conference call at a time. So, he did what desperate creatives do—he picked up a camera and started shooting.

No training. No mentorship. Just raw hunger and a good eye. He'd show up at our events and capture these moments that made our influencers look like Greek gods. High ISO, every vein popping, shadows carved like marble. If you go back and look at any fitness influencer from the early to mid 2010s, you'll recognize the style immediately. Ludwig was one of the guys who helped define it, and after a certain point, everyone else was just copying him. Or trying, at least.

Here's the part that still pisses me off, though: Ludwig shot 99% of the photos that made SHREDZ what it was, and Arvin didn't want to pay him. Not a dime. In Arvin's mind, Ludwig should have been grateful for the "exposure." I'd watch this guy work eighteen-hour days at our events, capturing the exact shots that would drive millions in sales, and then watch him eat ramen and lug his equipment around in an old beater.

So I did what I had to do. I'd slip him cash from my personal account. Not loans—payments. Because even back then, I understood that loyalty isn't bought, it's earned through reciprocal respect. When we'd go to the big fitness expos, I'd make sure Ludwig was there, credentials and all. I'll never forget the Olympia where he walked into the convention center and saw his photo of Joey Swoll blown up thirty feet tall. Ludwig just stopped in the middle of the floor and cried. How could he not? How many creatives get to see their work in a form that's *literally* larger than life and displayed in a place of honor?

After I left SHREDZ, Ludwig left Verizon to chase the creative dream, ended up at a marketing agency that promised him the world and delivered nothing. Then he went back to T-Mobile because bills don't pay themselves. Got laid off in some corporate restructuring. Tried banking, of all things. Imagine trying to explain aperture settings to a guy in a suit who only cares about interest rates. As you can probably imagine, he was miserable.

So, when I started rebuilding with AKG Creative, Ludwig was one of my first calls.

"I don't know if I can keep up with you," he said.

That honesty? That's exactly why I needed him. See, Ludwig's superpower isn't just design—though the man can make a trash bag look like a luxury item if you give him five minutes in Photoshop. His superpower is that he'll tell you the truth even when it costs him. In a world full of yes-men and mercenaries, Ludwig is the guy who'll say, "This isn't working" or "We need to slow down" or "That client is going to destroy us." On top of that (and maybe even because of it) Ludwig is intensely loyal. That's a big part of why he stuck around at SHREDZ for so long, even when it was painfully obvious that he was getting a raw deal. He just felt so connected to Arvin, our influencers, and, of course, me.

That kind of loyalty is a rare and beautiful thing. It's also something you must be careful not to exploit as a founder. Like I said, the key is to help people find their superpower, harness it, and ultimately own it. When you exploit people like Arvin was doing, it chips away at their confidence. That, in turn, hurts their ability to harness their superpower, and it makes fully owning it virtually impossible. Sure, you may be able to save yourself a dollar on talent today, but you're robbing yourself of millions tomorrow.

Case in point, Ludwig now serves as our brand architect. Not just the guy who makes things pretty, but the guy who understands that every pixel has a job. When our CPG clients come in with packaging that looks like it was designed in Microsoft Paint, Ludwig doesn't just redesign it. He rebuilds their entire visual language from the ground up. Brand guidelines that make sense even if you don't have a creative bone in your body. Color systems that work across print and digital. Typography *you can actually read* that still leaves a lasting impression. He's the guy who can look at a protein powder label and tell you exactly why it's failing on the shelf, then fix it.

Of course, here's what really sets Ludwig apart: he's been in the trenches. He knows what it's like to have your work stolen, your value dismissed, your talent wasted in corporate purgatory. So, when he works with our clients—whether they're scrappy startups or established brands trying to reinvent themselves—he brings that empathy. He doesn't just deliver assets. He delivers understanding. I've watched him spend hours explaining to a founder why their "minor tweak" would destroy six months of brand building. I've watched him fight for junior designers to get credit on projects. I've watched him turn down easy money because the client wanted something that would embarrass everyone involved. That's not just design. That's character.

And unlike those SHREDZ days where loyalty was a one-way street, here it flows both ways. We're proud to have Ludwig as our Chief Brand Officer, finally doing the work he was meant to do.

Now, the funny thing about my next cofounder is that he has almost the opposite story. Unlike with Ludwig, I had to convince Jason Aron to join us over the course of *years*. See, Jason had built Malka Media from nothing into the go-to production house for every major network. Showtime boxing documentaries, celebrity profiles, the works. Their IMDB page reads like a greatest hits collection of premium content. Jason and his team were creating content you've definitely seen, even if you didn't know they were behind it.

I first met Jason when SHREDZ became Malka's client. We needed video work that didn't look like it was shot in someone's garage, and Malka delivered. But what struck me wasn't just the quality—it was how Jason thought about storytelling. While everyone else was focused on making things "viral," Jason was focused on making things *matter*. The man had already directed the most popular documentary in Netflix history at the time—a *Back to the Future* retrospective he self-funded and Kickstarted because nobody else believed in it. He won Webbies. Shot drone footage for *A Quiet Place* among other things. This wasn't some hungry kid looking for his break. This was a guy who'd already made it.

So when Malka got acquired by a Chinese private equity firm and they started firing all the expensive talent—aka everyone actually good at their jobs—I saw my opportunity.

"Jason, come build a new Malka under my agency," I told him.

"Hmm, I'm good," he said.

Six months later: "Jason, the offer still stands."

"I'm still good."

A year later: "Jason, seriously."

"Ankur, come on man, I'm fine."

The thing about Jason's superpower is that it's not just creative vision—though he can see a story arc in a spreadsheet if you give him enough coffee. It's that he has access to talent nobody else can touch. The editors who cut primetime commercials. The cinematographers who shoot prestige television. The colorists who can make reality TV look like cinema. When Jason calls, they answer. Not because he pays the most, but because he's Jason Aron, and working with him means working on something that matters.

After my wedding in 2023—which, by the way, cost me three hundred grand and burned through every favor I had—I hit a dry spell. Four months, no business for AKG Creative. The kind of drought where you start wondering if maybe you peaked already. That's when I started hiring Jason's team for small projects. Three grand here, five grand there. Testing the waters. Then a twenty-grand project. Then another. Then another.

"Okay," Jason finally said, "let's have a real conversation."

See, Jason had been watching me rebuild. Not from a distance—from inside the machine, project by project. He'd seen me deliver when I had no right to deliver. He'd seen me keep my word when keeping it cost me money I didn't have. Most importantly, he'd seen me build systems that didn't depend on any one person's genius, including mine.

"What happens when my division outperforms yours?" he asked when he finally agreed to come aboard.

"Then you'll get a bigger piece," I said.

He laughed. "You know I just helped build a $100 million media company, right?"

"And you know I built a $125 million brand house, right?"

The difference between Jason and Ludwig isn't just their journeys—it's their wiring. Ludwig will sacrifice everything for a project he truly believes in. Jason needs to respect you before he'll even show up. Ludwig's loyalty comes from the heart. Jason's comes from the head. Ludwig will tell you the truth to protect you from yourself. Jason will tell you the truth because lying is inefficient.

Together, they're perfect. Ludwig obsesses over pixels. Jason obsesses over story arcs. Ludwig fights for what's right. Jason fights for what works. And when they disagree—which is often—magic happens. Because that tension, that push and pull between heart and head, between loyalty and logic, between beauty and business—that's where great work lives. Not to say one approach is creative and the other is not. *They both are.* They're just creative in different ways and at different scales. Ludwig is more micro, Jason is more macro, and you absolutely need both.

Speaking of Jason's division is projected to break $5 million this year. Not because he's grinding eighteen-hour days like we did at SHREDZ, but because he knows how to make every hour count.

Now, up until this point I've been talking about Ludwig and Jason like they're all under the same roof at AKG Creative. That is technically true, but remember, that's the holding company. And yes, as you might imagine, their work weaves into what we're doing at Flexwork Studios in a major way. Still, to truly make the most of their talents, I had to open up a new agency that would be under a new umbrella. One that can take a promising founder and transform them into an unforgettable character in their industry. One that can *create* the influencers we need to promote all our CPG brands. One that lets us not only TELL the story but BE the story as we apply all these same tools to ourselves.

Enter Youngry.

The name comes from a simple premise: Young in Spirit, Hungry in Ambition. The first part is important because we've all had our rough patches. You've seen pretty much all of mine, and you've gotten a glimpse of Ludwig's and Jason's. Still, in true Rogue Visionary fashion, we haven't let those seasons snuff out our passion. Far from it. For each of us, our scar tissue is our resume, and we wear it with pride. Likewise, we are Hungry in *Ambition* not because we're gluttons for punishment. We've all had dozens of offramps we could have taken in life—shortcuts to an "easy" life that would have meant "good" money and plenty of nods of approval from friends and family. We've driven right past those offramps, and will continue to do so, because we all know we're not wired that way. Easy is death. "Good enough" is the grave. None of us could live with ourselves if we weren't squeezing everything we could out of our superpowers.

So that's what we do at Youngry, and that's our invitation and *expectation* for every new team member we bring in. Do not apply if you plan to coast. Do not apply if you're looking for "safety" or "security." In case it's not already obvious, I do look out for my people, and I'll have even more to say about that in a future chapter. Still, do not mistake that for coddling.

Youngry is not here to keep you out of danger. Youngry is here to make you dangerous. And if that sounds exciting to you, we'd love to have you.

For now, though, let's zoom back out and take a look at the full ecosystem.

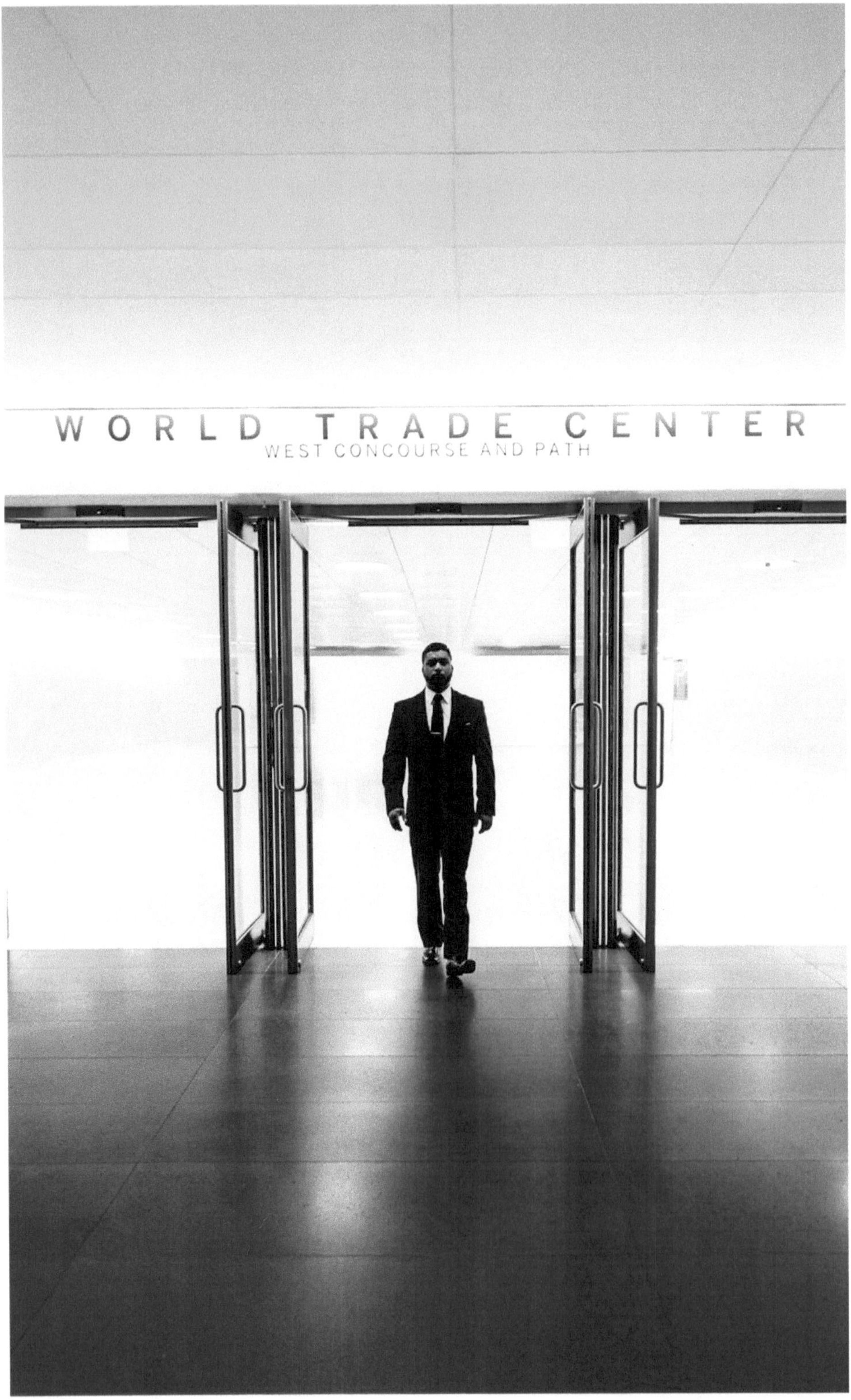
WORLD TRADE CENTER
WEST CONCOURSE AND PATH

Chapter 12
Why You Must Delegate or Die

I always think it's adorable when I see someone call themselves a "serial entrepreneur". Because that implies each business is "part of a series". They come one after the other. It kind of has the same ring as "serial monogamist", in fact.

That is never how my businesses have operated. I also have yet to meet a single high-level entrepreneur who operates that way. Sure, there are mom and pop shops that slowly but surely build their way up into the low millions over half a lifetime. But the people who get to put their names on buildings? The ones who get to steer the course of history? The ones who *install* the people you *think* are in power? They don't get there by baby-stepping through one business at a time.

Heck, I would never have escaped my hometown if I operated that way. Remember how I was DJ'in, building websites, and dealing weed all before I graduated high school? Remember how my parents worked multiple jobs just to rebuild the lives they had back in India (and reach even higher)? That's not because we were "passionate" or "driven" to do all those things. That was *math*. Either we learned to juggle many different things, or we would never hit our goals. That's it.

So, for one thing, understand that it's normal for a Rogue Visionary to have a lot of different irons in the fire. If that's you, then great. You're in good company. Two, now that you've accepted that this isn't going to change, we need to talk about how to manage it all without going insane.

At time of writing, there are roughly 200 different brands under the Youngry umbrella. Like I said before, some of those are brands that we created in-house. Some of them are start-ups that we are accelerating. Some of them are legacy corporations looking to leap to the cutting edge of modern media. Some of them are mom and pop shops. Some of them are publicly traded companies with multi-million-dollar valuations. On top of all that, they cut across a wide swath of industries too. Health supplements (of course), but also biotech, legal services, restaurants, snacks, culinary, financial services, and plenty of personal brands.

At any given time, each of those brands needs something different. Youngry is responsible for meeting all those needs, and I am responsible for Youngry. I am *100% responsible* for Youngry, and therefore all those brands, even though my partners each hold minority shares.

You may have thought it was "cute" when I talked about building my superhero team in the last chapter. I am telling you it's a matter of life and death. It would not be possible to maintain that client list if I was doing everything myself. It wouldn't even be possible if I was *managing* everything myself. Make no mistake, I still do plenty of "management" in the traditional sense. Still, there are countless decisions that need to be made and executed upon every single day. There's no way that could happen if every little thing needed my personal review and sign off.

So let's talk about the difference between *responsibility* and *control*, which is the #1 thing I see killing entrepreneurs at this stage or earlier. (Sometimes literally). Taking *control* is when you micro-manage. It's when you require every decision in the business to come from you or go through you. It's tempting, especially in the beginning, because you *can* get a lot done that way. You *can* create and maintain a high level of quality…at first. The problem is that, for one thing, you become the bottleneck. I don't care how smart you are or how hard you can grind; there WILL come a point where there are too many decisions for your brain to process in a single day. Two, and this is actually a much greater danger, your taking control is a recipe for disaster when it comes to team dynamics.

When you have a controlling CEO at the helm of the business, here's what happens: C-level talent completely checks out. They start acting like robots because they realize there's no thinking required of them, so they don't bother. Not good robots, for the record. Rusty, clanky, busted robots that require endless repair and maintenance. B-level talent doesn't check out, per se.

Instead, they turn political. They recognize that the CEO's approval is the one and only currency that matters, so they adjust their thinking and behavior accordingly. Quality of work and client satisfaction become distant secondary goals. What really matters is pleasing the CEO and *being seen as* the most important part of the team.

The real tragedy, of course, is what happens to A-level talent. They don't check out, nor do they turn political. By definition, they're so obsessed with doing great work that they refuse to make those compromises. So instead, they either rebel or they *leave.* And as crazy as it might sound, rebellion is actually the better option. At least that way you have a chance to reconcile with them and keep their genius under your roof. Sadly, most of the time they won't even bother rebelling. They'll just leave and take their genius somewhere else, most likely to one of your competitors. Sometimes this happens when a B-level team member discovers their true superpower, harnesses it, and becomes A-level. For the people who already *are* A-level talent? Often, they can sniff it out as early as the first interview, and they'll bounce before you can even make them an offer.

I know there's a certain kind of reader who's going to grit their teeth as they read this. They don't want to give up control. They like control. One could even argue they're addicted to it. I know because I used to be that guy, as we'll get to a bit later on. So let me tackle your main objection right now: *I am not asking you to lower your standards*. You probably *think* that's what I mean when I talk about giving up control, but it's not. That would mean giving up *responsibility*.

I am not asking you to give up responsibility. I am asking you to take *more* responsibility.

Taking responsibility means you are "able to answer" for something. It's right there in the word: when something goes wrong, you are the one who *responds*. To do that, you can't get so fixated on the work, like the controlling CEO does. Instead, you need to obsess over the people. After all, they're there to do the work for you, right? Isn't that why you hired them? Isn't that why you're paying them? So why not get out of the way and let them do it?

Ah, that's right: it's because you don't trust them. And you don't trust them because you've never given them the opportunity to BE trustworthy. The only way they can be trustworthy is if *they* carry legitimate responsibility within their work. They must be able to make a decision, execute it on it, track the results, decide whether it was a success or a failure, and proceed from there. If they cannot complete that whole loop without you in the room? Then they don't really have responsibility. They're merely carrying out your control. They may even be *reliable* in carrying out your control, but that's not the same as being trustworthy. If you have a coffee grinder that perfectly grinds your coffee every time, do you "trust" it? No, it's just reliable.

So let's get the obvious out of the way: micromanaging does not work because it does not let people have responsibility. Hiring someone else to micromanage on your behalf doesn't work for the same reason. Does that mean the goal is to just hire people and let them do whatever they want? No, of course not. As I've said before, having SOPs is essential if you ever want to scale the business. But those SOPs should never feel like a set of shackles. Instead, they should provide the baseline for effective work. At its core, an SOP is a document that says, "Here is the process that has worked for us many times in the past. So when in doubt, just follow this process."

What about all the tiny adjustments you need per-client? Heck, what about being able to innovate and actually stay ahead of the curve? That's where bringing on the right talent comes in. A-level talent will do all that naturally. B-Level talent needs more handholding, but if you put them next to A-level talent they'll want to keep pace. And C-Level talent? Only they can decide when they're going to have their next breakthrough, but in the meantime, they can mop up whatever the A and B-level talent need to delegate. As long as they can feel useful and get paid, that's all they need for now.

Of course, that's assuming the work is all happening under normal conditions. What about when a critical piece of technology breaks? What about when a client completely ghosts you and now you've got a team full of idle hands? What about a critical team member leaves and everyone else has to fill the gap? And hey, why stop at the office? What happens when somebody has a sick loved one at home? What if they're going through a bad break up or even a divorce? What if they've got three different girlfriends and all three of them show up to the office looking for an explanation?

Guess what, Rogue Visionary: you're responsible for all that too.

Not fair? Too bad. Until the robots have taken over literally everything, business happens through people and people have problems. Personal problems. Gnarly, sticky problems that don't magically disappear the minute they set foot in the office. No, you cannot run around solving all those problems for them. Yes, it is important to maintain healthy professional boundaries. *But the least you can do is equip your people to fight back.*

For example, any time a team member needs a new tool to get their work done? I pay for it through the company, no questions asked. There's no "approval process" to check in. If *I* think it's worth the money. I trust them. If they say they need it, I want them to have it, and I *don't* want them stressing about the cost. Yes, even if they are in a contractor or vendor position where it would make sense (and be legally justified) for them to pay for their own tools. The point is not to worry about the legal CYA mindset. *The point is supporting my people.*

Likewise, if someone has a sudden financial emergency and they need me to work something out with payroll? Done. I don't care if it wasn't my fault. I don't care if they were perfectly managing their finances or not. I am responsible for them. And I can tell you, from a purely selfish, cold-blooded perspective, that it's *cheaper* to operate this way than the alternative. The better your talent is, the more expensive it is to replace them. Why would I let a personal crisis take them off the board if I have the power to give them a lifeline? Plus, word gets around. When the rest of the team sees you stick your neck out for a team member in trouble? That does wonders for morale. That allows EVERYONE on the team to be a little more bold and a little more fearless, knowing that there's a safety net if they ever truly need it.

None of this is to say I'm some kind of saint, nor that I run my business like a charity. The flip side of all of this is that I expect everyone on my team to give me their best every single day. And

I accept just their absolute best *for today only*. I expect them to keep developing their abilities and even themselves regardless of anything I say. And when I do see any kind of flaw in their work, it's my responsibility to say something *immediately* and *directly*. No waiting for them to figure it out on their own. No tiptoeing around to protect their feelings. Honestly, A-level talent hates that shit anyway. To them, you trying to play nice only gets in the way of doing great work.

Now, if it sounds like my business advice is starting to bleed into personal development, that's because it is. And if that makes you uncomfortable, good. That means we're finally digging into the *real* reason people get into entrepreneurship. The real reason why we keep going even when it sucks. The real motivation and the real reward. And I've got way, *way* more to say about it in the next chapter.

Chapter 13
The True Definition of "Alpha"

Before we dive back into definitions, let me show you what "alpha" looks like in action.

One of our most exciting partners right now is a biotech company doing groundbreaking work in cellular and genetic therapy. Think stem-cell exosomes, allogeneic CDCs, and other therapies—not just as abstract science, but as real, scalable products with FDA engagement. Their therapies aren't just for symptoms; they're designed to actually influence regeneration and cellular communication. It's cutting-edge stuff, but also deeply human. To put it in perspective, they're working on tech that could help the body repair itself after heart failure or muscular degeneration—breakthroughs that move the entire healthcare narrative from reactive to regenerative.

Very science-y, I know. Even I lose track of all these terms sometimes. But the punchline is this: this is borderline *Star Trek* stuff. They are taking conditions that used to be "impossible" to manage and creating unheard of breakthroughs.

Case in point, one of the most promising applications is in the treatment of Duchenne Muscular Dystrophy (DMD)—a brutal and rare disease that slowly shuts down every muscle in the body, including the heart. Over the last few years, a clinical drug trial has helped many with DMD stabilize their health, giving them the opportunity to live and maintain independence for much longer. But now that drug is at risk of being pulled off the table—because of a bureaucratic technicality. That drug, of course, is an allogeneic cardio sphere-derived cell (aka a type of stem cell therapy), so we've been working with the families directly to campaign on behalf of the young men with DMD, both to support them and to demonstrate the power of these clinical solutions on a national scale.

Just last month, we flew out to California to shoot interview footage with several young men suffering from DMD. The first shoot was in San Diego, and the second one was in Santa Ana, which is two hours to the north. Both shoots were scheduled for the same day, mind you. By the time we reached the studio for the shoot in Santa Ana, everyone was tired already.

Still, we had a job to do. A job that could save the lives of the two young men we were interviewing—a pair of brothers living with DMD who have already lost their eldest to the same disease. So as soon as we got there, I found the biggest parking spot I could find for our media team and parked *myself* there until they caught up with us. While I was waiting, my friend and client Mark Awadalla came up to me in a mood. He was exhausted, like we all were, and immediately launched into a rant about timelines, budgets, and everything you might expect to be weighing on a high-level corporate executive. After all, he's the Chief Development Officer at a Biotechnology Company, the company responsible for the DMD treatment in question.

At first, I hit him back with some lighthearted grousing of my own. I even turned out my pockets to show that I know what it's like to have budgetary concerns. Still, I made no effort to try to prove him wrong or even prove me right. I just let him vent, since that's all he really needed. By the time we made it inside and sat down with the brothers, something had shifted. Not because I'd argued Mark out of his mood or given him some motivational speech. That's not how real leadership works. I'd just created the space for him to decompress, and now we had work to do. Important work. Life-or-death work, literally.

The moment Elijah, the older brother, started talking about his experience with DMD, everything else fell away. Budget concerns? Timeline stress? All that corporate noise just evaporated. Here was this young man, muscles failing him day by day, talking about hope with more conviction than most healthy people can muster on their best days. And when he mentioned how the therapeutic treatment had stabilized his brother's condition, how it had given his brother years he thought they'd lost and how he wished he was able to get the treatment himself—that's when I saw it happen.

Mark and I locked eyes across the room. No words. Just this moment of recognition: *we got it.* That one 30-second clip had made the whole shoot worth it. That one clip would have the power to go viral, wake people up, and fuel the grassroots campaign to get Congress to move on this issue. That's what it always comes down to when you're dealing with a rare disease like this. Politicians are incentivized to appeal to the *masses*, not a disease that affects about 1 in every 5,000 people. Therefore, when you can harness the attention of the masses and point it towards a campaign like this? That's when things change.

After the shoot, the boys went home with their father and the rest of us met up for dinner at a local BBQ spot. Even after such a long day, and all the ongoing pressure on his shoulders, Mark was a complete teddy bear. Just smiling and laughing and ordering us all way more food than we could actually finish.

That's what real alpha energy looks like. Not beating your chest about being in charge. Not making everyone know you're the boss. It's creating the conditions where everyone—from the exhausted film crew to the stressed executive to the kids fighting for their lives—feels safe enough to do what needs to be done. I won't say I got *zero* credit. I did get paid and get some tasty barbecue, after all.

Still, the level of "credit" you get for being a true alpha is never quite as much as what you put in. Not if you're trying to measure it pound for pound. In fact, your influence becomes kind of invisible as a true alpha. People just feel safe, energized, and inspired around you even if they can't explain why.

You want to know what's exhausting? Watching guys try to perform "alpha" like it's a Halloween costume they bought off Amazon. They walk into rooms trying to own them. They interrupt conversations to make sure everyone knows they're important. They name-drop, they peacock, they turn every interaction into a competition they have to win.

Those aren't alphas. Those are betas in disguise, desperately trying to convince themselves and everyone else that they matter.

Truth be told, I was that guy at one point—but I dropped that twenty years ago. Because here's what those costume-party alphas don't understand: the second you have to announce your dominance, you've already lost it. You either have it or you don't. And if you have it, you don't need to advertise. Back in my twenties, sure, I'd walk into clubs with my DJ equipment, making sure everyone knew I was somebody. I'd drop my revenue numbers into casual conversation. I'd make sure people knew about my connections, my wins, my importance. It was exhausting—not just for everyone around me, but for me. Being "on" all the time, maintaining that facade, making sure the mask never slipped? That's not power. That's performance anxiety.

So how did I make the switch from beta in disguise to true alpha?

Two words: scar tissue.

The fake alpha thinks he's bulletproof. He needs to prove it constantly because deep down, he's never been truly tested. He's like a fresh black belt who's never been in a real fight—all technique, no experience with chaos. So he overcompensates. He's loud because he's afraid of being ignored. He's aggressive because he's afraid of being challenged. He dominates conversations because he's afraid of silence.

The real alpha? He's quiet because he has nothing to prove. He's been through the SHREDZ collapse, the basement, the Pittsburgh prison cell. He's had half his mustache fall out from stress and grown it back from confidence. He doesn't need to tell you he can handle pressure—his presence tells you he's already handled worse than whatever's in front of him now.

I build companies like I'm building kingdoms. And in a kingdom, the king doesn't get to clock out at five. The king doesn't get to say, "That's not my department." Everything is your department. Every problem is your problem. Every person's struggle becomes your puzzle to solve. Whether or not Ludwig's kids eats is my responsibility. Whether or not Jason can sleep at night is my responsibility. That's not an exaggeration. When you're truly alpha—when you're truly building something—everyone becomes your responsibility.

Most people hear that and think it sounds like hell. Those people will never be true alphas. They'll never be kings. Because being king isn't about sitting on a throne while everyone serves you. It's about serving everyone while carrying the weight of the throne.

Let me tell you about real presence. Shah Rukh Khan, the biggest Bollywood actor in the world, has 5,000 to 10,000 people living outside his house at any given moment. Not visiting. *Living* there. Just hoping to catch a glimpse of him. When Shah Rukh Khan walks into a room, people go silent. Not from fear. Not from intimidation. From presence. He's "the kind of guy that makes you believe that you could do what he did," as one comedian perfectly described it. He landed in Mumbai with a suitcase and nothing else, built an empire, and somehow makes you feel like you could do it too.

That's the difference between demanding attention and commanding it. The betas demand it—they need you to look at them, acknowledge them, validate them. True alphas command it simply by existing. They don't need to raise their voice because the room naturally quiets when they speak. They don't need to dominate because everyone naturally defers.

I don't know if I have that level of aura yet. But I try to emulate it. Not by copying his moves or studying his interviews. By understanding that true power makes other people feel powerful, not powerless. Entertainment is one way of doing that. My way of doing that is through business. And let me tell you, after all I've been through, there are very few things that I don't know about business.

That's not bragging. That's scar tissue talking. I've been through lawsuits, algorithm changes, partnership betrayals, biotech layoffs, and five complete restarts. I've built up to nine figures and lost it all. I've gone from penthouses to basements, from millions to negative millions, from having answers to having nothing but questions.

You know what all that trauma gives you? The ability to make other people feel safe.

When a client comes to me panicking about their first lawsuit, I can say, "I've been through twelve at once." When a founder tells me they're out of money, I can say, "I've been $1.8 million in the hole." When someone's partnership is falling apart, I can show them the exact clause that cost me $50 million. Battle-tested versus untested—that's the real difference. The untested leader makes everyone nervous because they're nervous. They're figuring it out in real-time, and everyone can feel it. The battle-tested leader has seen worse, survived worse, and everyone can feel that too. They relax because they know you can handle whatever comes next.

Back in high school, I figured something out that changed everything: you don't need to be president to have presidential power. I was running for president of all these clubs—Student Government, DECA, Debate Team, the South Asian Alliance, whatever organization would have me. Then a friend pulled me aside and asked, "Why do you want to be president?"

"To create change," I said.

"Then why be president? Plant the president instead. Make someone who owes you the president. You get all the power, none of the paperwork."

Genius. Pure genius. Real alphas don't need the title. They don't need their name on the door or the business card that says "CEO" or the seat at the head of the table. They need influence, and influence flows through relationships, not org charts. Speaking of which, everything I'm saying about being an "alpha" applies equally to the term "entrepreneur". It's not a title you claim. It's a reality you create or you don't.

Entrepreneurship is still defined as having the audacity to think your way to solve problems is better than the solutions that are out there. That's it. Either you look at the world and see better ways to do things, or you don't. Either you act on those visions, or you don't. There's no middle ground, no "aspiring entrepreneur," no "entrepreneurial mindset" without entrepreneurial action.

Most of all, this applies to being a Rogue Visionary. So let's determine, once and for all, if *you* are a Rogue Visionary.

Chapter 14
Your "Homework"

So now you've seen it all. The ups, the downs, and everything in between.

By the way, if you're reading this on or near publication day, I just turned 40. Yes, it was a very heavy cake. Yes, the candles nearly burnt the house down. Hilarious.

Is this where teenage Ankur thought I would be at 40? No. He thought I would be building hospitals by now. But here I am, and I wouldn't trade the scar tissue for anything. Honestly, if I could bring teenage Ankur forward in time to see what I'm doing now, I don't think he'd care that much about the money. I don't think he'd be judging me by my car or my house or shoes.

I think he'd see the work we're doing for those young men with DMD and understand exactly what I'm doing. Fixing god's mistakes, one campaign at a time, like I set out to do all those years ago. People say "don't let it change you" when you go through a rough patch, but I think that's missing the point. We're *supposed* to grow and change. You can't not be changed by failure. The same goes for success. And if it weren't for the hefty, mixed-up brew of both, I wouldn't be equipped to do what I'm doing now.

So, let's return to that original question, the one question you have to answer for yourself if you're going to write a book like this: can I turn someone into a Rogue Visionary if they're not one already?

No. No, you can't. No, I can't. No book, or author, can.

Does that mean this book was pointless? Or, at best, a vanity project? No. In fact, this book has a very important purpose, one that goes way beyond building my personal brand. (Although I'm not *not* doing that as well.) The point of this book is to get you to take a pledge. Not an easy pledge, though it is a simple one. In fact, it's so simple that you might be tempted to look at it and say, "Sure, whatever." Or, at least, you would be tempted to say "okay I'll do it" even if I had presented the pledge on its own, without context. Now you do have context. Now you know exactly where I'm coming from. Now you know there's no wishful thinking or naivety involved here.

So here is my pledge:

"I, Ankur K Garg, hereby swear to abandon all weakness, to reach finish lines, to trust in my work ethic, to honor those who inspire me and support all those who follow me. I swear that I will never accept procrastination as an option, and I will always maintain my resolve. When I'm finished, I will be remembered as the Marketing Guru of my generation."

I picked the title of "Marketing Guru" because that's what I do. *And who I am.* For you, it could be anything. I wouldn't dare try to pick that for you. What I will say is that this pledge is all you need. Seriously. You don't need another "playbook" or safety net. If you truly are a Rogue Visionary, you will be the one *writing* the playbooks and *building* the safety nets.

Swearing the pledge is not what makes you a Rogue Visionary, of course. All it does is unleash your inner Rogue Visionary *if you have one.* And just to make sure you actually have one in there, I'm going to give you every reason not to be a Rogue Visionary.

You do not need to become a Rogue Visionary to make a lot of money. What is "a lot" of money, anyway? Have you ever taken the time to actually define that for yourself? You should. Whenever you get the chance, sit down and write out the most ridiculous lifestyle you can imagine for yourself. List out where you live, what kind of car you drive, how many vacations you take, your hobbies, everything. Then price it out, the same way my mom and I did for building and operating a hospital. I promise you, the most extravagant thing you can imagine is *nothing* compared to running a hospital. Plus, there are probably parts of that vision you could buy for yourself *today.* So start there and work your way up. Honestly, you'll probably be totally content before you get halfway through the list. Especially since most "luxuries" really only feel special the first time.

You do not need to become a Rogue Visionary to have freedom. Again, this is a question of defining your terms. What does "freedom" mean to you? If it means not having to work, congrats, you are *not* a Rogue Visionary. There are countless ways to survive and even thrive (relatively speaking) as a lazy person. If you want to be lazy then fine, go all in. Nobody is asking you to become a Rogue Visionary. In fact…

You MUST not become a Rogue Visionary if you want to be popular. This is coming from the guy who literally invented influencer marketing. My most charitable interpretation of influencer culture is that it is shallow, stupid, and fueled by greed at every level. Want to blow up on Instagram? Be a hot chick and stick your ass directly in the camera. Want to blow up on YouTube? Rent a sports car or a mansion for an afternoon and pretend you and your boys all bought Bitcoin early. The fastest, simplest, and ultimately cheapest way to become popular is to fake it. We all know this. It hasn't been a secret for years. We all know the booties are plastic and the cars are rented. We don't care. We keep watching because, for the 15 seconds of attention we'll give you, we are using you as a vessel to act out our own fantasies. Gross? Arguably. But that's just how popularity works and *always has.* Social media has only amplified it.

And if you think you need to be a Rogue Visionary to get laid? *Please.* You give me an afternoon on the actual Jersey Shore, and I'll find you a guy who is technically homeless but still getting more play than the five richest guys I know *combined*. That's just game. All it takes is a little bit of practice and some semi-regular bathing. Honestly, depending on who you ask, that second part is optional.

Earlier in the book, I mentioned "off ramps" on the path to success. These are exactly what I mean by that. These are the "off ramps" people take in life. I don't blame them. In fact, I think you SHOULD take the off ramps if you're not a true Rogue Visionary at heart. The world does not benefit from you scraping along trying to be something you're not. If you're not a Rogue Visionary, there are countless ways you can serve the Rogue Visionaries of the world and get pretty much whatever you want in return.

Ah…but did that just piss you off?

Seriously, does it make you feel some type of way when I talk about you serving someone else? Do you get a twitch in your eye? A twinge in your neck? A certain, ahem, puckering somewhere? Better yet, do you find yourself vaguely disgusted by all those "off ramps"? Not because you don't want the same things, but because you can't stand the idea of *settling* for them.

Or maybe it's as simple as the old Robert Frost quote:

> *Two roads diverged in a wood, and I—*
>
> *I took the one less traveled by,*
>
> *And that has made all the difference.*

You know, deep down, that you're never going to accomplish everything you could if you keep following other people's path. And yes, you will need to go alone *at first*. Maybe that excites you too. Maybe it scares you. Maybe both. This is where the "Rogue" half comes in, after all.

But there's a difference between being a leader and being a loner. If you go down that path without leading anyone else that way? Then it dies with you. Whatever treasures you discover will sink back into the earth, and life as usual will continue for everyone else. However, if you can step up and seize the "Visionary" half, you can lead other people down the path. No, they will never understand the full weight you're carrying for them. They will never understand the choice you had to make at the outset.

Still, when you find the treasure, you'll have someone to share it with. Dozens of people. Hundreds, even. Thousands. Millions. And you'll have the satisfaction of knowing *you are the reason* why everyone gets to celebrate.

Is that enough for you? Can you be satisfied with knowing you have created something great, even before the money comes, even when there are fires raging all around you, and even when the crowds don't understand it YET?

Then you are a Rogue Visionary, and there's nothing I can give you that's more powerful than that. So don't wait another second for me or anyone else to give you the answers. You don't need answers. *You need scar tissue*. The more scar tissue you earn, the more people will recognize you as the alpha you are and follow you. Abandon all fear.

Take the pledge.

THE PLEDGE

"I, _____, hereby swear to abandon all weakness, to reach finish lines, to trust in my work ethic, to honor those who inspire me and support all those who follow me. I swear that I will never accept procrastination as an option, and I will always maintain my resolve. When I'm finished, I will be remembered as the ___ _____ of my generation."

ABOUT THE AUTHOR

Ankur K. Garg is a battle-tested brand builder, creative strategist, and operator who has scaled dozens of consumer-packaged brands to millions in revenue.

Before founding Youngry and launching a new wave of DTC growth brands, Ankur pioneered influencer marketing when the word "influencer" barely existed. He didn't just ride trends—he saw them coming, built infrastructure around them, and turned raw vision into revenue at scale. Along the way, he's faced lawsuits, betrayal, burnout, and the brutal weight of leadership. He's also helped rebuild brands from zero, guided companies through 8-figure exits, and served as the engine behind some of the most viral marketing campaigns of the last decade.

Today, Ankur serves as a fractional CMO, advisor, speaker, and founder of Youngry Media—a creative growth studio that builds movements, not just brands.

This is his first book.
It won't be his last.

Follow his work at www.ankurkgarg.com
Connect on Social Media @ankurkgarg

youngry

Published in the United States by Youngry
623 Morris Avenue, Springfield, NJ 07081

ABOUT YOUNGRY PUBLISHING

Youngry Publishing exists to amplify voices that build, break, and rebuild. We publish real stories from real founders—not sanitized bios or ghostwritten hype.

We believe the future belongs to those who create it.
That means telling the truth, not the trend.
That means highlighting raw lessons, not just polished wins.
That means giving a platform to the builders, breakers, and comeback kings who know what it's like to bet everything on a vision.

If you're a founder, operator, or visionary with a story the world *needs* to hear—not just wants to hear—Youngry Publishing was built for you.

We don't publish books for the bookshelf.
We publish books that spark movements.

youngry.com/publishing
For submissions, inquiries, and partnerships, email: publishing@youngry.com

www.ingramcontent.com/pod-product-compliance
Lightning Source LLC
Chambersburg PA
CBHW040926190426
43197CB00033B/107